It's a Bedroom, Not a Boardroom
Protect Your Relationship from being Damaged by Business Tools

Lois V. Nightingale, Ph.D

Published by:
Nightingale Rose Publications
16960 East Bastanchury Road, Suite J
Yorba Linda, California 92886

Acknowledgements:
I want to thank Dave and Baz for their constant belief that I could finish this project. And a special debt of gratitude to business owners and CEOs who have courageously shared with me their challenges and successes in the boardrooms and the bedrooms of their lives, TB, MD and MM, among so many others
All my writing peers in Los Angeles Writers and Poets Collative, Jack, Minda, and all the Wednesday morning bunch of hooligans.
My wonderful life partner, Mike, and all the kids, Harry, Teddi, Nick and Spencer.

Book Design by Baz Here and Lois Nightingale
Author Photo by Baz Here

It's a Bedroom, Not a Boardroom: Protect You Relationship from Being Damaged by Business Tools

ISBN-13 978-1-889755-05-2
Library of Congress Copyright, 2016 1-2662612954
© Lois V. Nightingale

Summary: A self-help book for couples who struggle with bringing work-style communication home.

Disclaimer
This book is designed to provide information in regard to the subject matter covered. It is not designed to take the place of professional counseling. If someone is having a particularly difficult time handling their emotional or mental concerns it is important to seek professional help. The family members and ancestors of Dr. Nightingale referred to in this book are based on real people, all other characters or references are fictionalized. Any similarities to real people are coincidental and unintended.

Table of Contents

Introduction

I have to admit I've had a life-long love/hate relationship with both business and romance. In gathering stories from both my father and mother's sides of the family tree, I've found it must flow through my veins.

In this book, my intention is to give the reader a larger picture of healthy personal communication, in contrast to great business communication. I give the reader specific examples, exercises, and stories about business and building intimate relationships. In America, the history of financial enterprise cannot be completely severed from the history of religion and the support of family.

I was brought up in a religion that taught all our treasure should be stored in heaven and the pursuit of earthly wealth was sinful. Door-to-door sales calls were exclusively for the purpose of harvesting souls for the hereafter. With chaos at home, and twelve years of fundamentalist church school, I was given similarly confusing instructions about romantic love and partnership. At fourteen, I decided to pursue the study of psychology and try to make sense out of a paradoxical world.

I've learned over the years how to cherish ambition, even though many of my prized endeavors fizzled to the ground after partial launches. I'll give more of these stories as examples in this book later, but here are a couple life changing ones:

After a year of research, finding sponsors and completing challenging negotiations with medical insurance companies, I opened an innovative postpartum depression unit in a local psychiatric hospital. After serving new mothers and their infants for only a few months, the hospital (under an intense federal investigation) sold to a competitor. The new owners promptly closed my hard-earned, specialized unit. I was financially devastated when I jumped the gun by founding an integrative medicine center with a staff of twelve without doing local market research in my conservative community, and I also failed to drug test the office staff handling my money. As with everyone in business, there have been numerous other adventures, but I'm now the proud owner of two successful enterprises.

After three and a half years, my first relationship became physically and emotionally abusive. To end the relationship, I hitched a U-Haul to my green, manual transmission Gremlin and moved 400 miles away, reevaluated everything I believed in and started a new life. When the fifteen-year relationship with my husband, a business owner, ended in divorce, I wasn't sure I could find the energy to return to the dating scene as a single mom, much less scrape up the hope that I could find a real peer and partner. I am now in a loving, long-term relationship with a man (also a business owner) who is my best friend, lover and greatest cheerleader.

In this book, I want to share with you what I have found on my journey. My hope is that you'll find practical answers here, especially if you're one of those naturally ambitious and driven individuals, but find you still feel lonely and invisible when you're with your partner.

What I noticed as a psychologist:

My private therapy practice is in a quiet city in Orange County, California. In 2006, it was rated the highest median household income city in the United States and continues to be in the top ten. The sprawling yards, high-end cars, private schools, exotic vacations, and absence of survival stress, do not tell the whole story of what goes on inside many of these beautiful homes.

The emotional pain and confusion revealed in my office seems incongruent with the career success of most of my clients. They are often baffled at the chaos in their homes, especially when they seem to have everything they thought would bring them happiness.

They are determined and ambitious. Many come from humble backgrounds. They share stories of sacrifice. They're dedicated to creating financial security for their families. They define themselves as successful in all the ways we've been taught to define success.

They're educated, respected, world-traveled, and influential. They trust themselves and their skills for building success, yet they find themselves on the verge of ending another relationship, financing another divorce, or facing the thing they hate most: failure.

The affluent elite are used to taking care of problems. Most of them have never been in therapy before. When trouble showed up in the past, they wrangled it into submission, usually at a profit. It's with ambivalence and reluctance that they find themselves on my couch.

It's as if they're trying to navigate around New York City with a map of Chicago. The map is accurate, detailed, useful, but when applied to a different city it's misleading, even dangerous. Finding one's way around with an inappropriate map is impossible, yet that's what numerous couples do when they apply business strategies to their personal intimate relationships.

This is not a business book--there are many great ones out there—and this not a traditional relationship book. This book is an instruction guide for people who've been using a great map, but in the wrong arena. This book provides new GPS coordinates and a useful map that will get you where you want to be on the relationship field.

How to get the most out of this book:

I suggest you keep a journal and do the exercises at the end of each chapter. The practice of finding the right words is important. You can even throw the pages away if you don't feel comfortable keeping them. It's the *process* of writing your new thoughts that's most important, not whether you keep what you write.
If you do decide to keep your journal writing, mark your calenda

six months from the day you finish the book. Revisit the book on that date and reread your writings. Be honest with yourself about how your new skills are progressing, and where you may have slipped back into old habits.

Learning any new skill takes work. This is even more true when you have to unlearn old patterns that you've practiced since you learned to talk. Be gentle with yourself and your partner if these concepts seem difficult at first. It does get easier, and soon your new communication skills will become second nature.

The exercises are designed to increase your knowledge of yourself and build your own communication skills. We can only change ourselves, but as I have often seen in therapy, one partner consistently responding a new way can change the entire dynamic of a relationship.

Make the information in this book come alive in your relationship, don't let it be just "one more self-help book." You deserve a vivacious, passionate, loving relationship. Take on that challenge today.

Chapter One

For the Love of Business

When I was working on my Ph.D., my dissertation was on temperament theory. I analyzed statistics correlating someone's strength of preference for a particular temperament with their ratings of self-confidence. My data explored the question: If a person has a well-defined temperament, might they also exhibit more qualities of self-esteem? There were some statistically significant findings, but what I found the most fascinating were the unique motivating drives behind the ambitious actions of each of the temperaments.

An Idealist, for instance, was motivated to be genuine in their career choice; not following their true purpose would seem like a failure. A Rational cared most about competency; work was about implementing ideas and being the expert. A Guardian was most driven by wanting to be of service. The Artisans were driven to have an impact. They have endless energy, and are about action in their vocations. To all of these folks, being appreciated for their decisiveness, organization, and practicality motivated them most in their work.

Any of the temperaments may be driven by their careers, but each is fueled by different goals. When someone has found work that is a particular fit for their temperament, everything else may seem harder by comparison. Those fortunate enough to have sought out and found work that's a true fit for themselves, may find they are re-energized by each new success. They may also shy away from arenas where they don't feel they can enjoy the same sense of accomplishment.

Current business entrepreneurs, who are passionate about their work, have given us things we never dreamed possible. However, to be respectful, many of the products and services that make our lives easier and more comfortable have come with price tags we'll never see. Many of those hard-working ground breakers found that when their business agendas were applied to their intimate relationships, devastating things happened. This doesn't have to be the case anymore.

No matter what the motivation was behind starting a business, it failed or succeeded based on its ability to stay competitive. When success or fail criteria are used to evaluate marriages we arrive at very strange conclusions. We've all heard, "Their marriage failed." All that is meant by this is, "They didn't make it to ''til death do us part'."

"Failure" of a marriage is a specific comment on separating before one person quits breathing. Nothing more. This defines marital "success" as one partner dying while still married. It may seem morbid, but it's the unconscious assumption behind many conversations about relationships.

Relationship success may be better defined as the *quality* of the partnership, not that it ended in a mortuary. Subjective success might be feeling special and important even when there are challenges to face in the relationship. It might be the certainty of connection even when you both want different things. Subjective failure might be feeling lonely and isolated even when you have someone right next to you. It might be always fearing rebuke or that the relationship is about to end.

These, of course, are much more difficult concepts to measure. Those who naturally think in business terms are more comfortable discussing objective measures. It's easier to talk about things that can be compared, researched, substantiated and tangibly defined. Even if it's hard to find the right words, most of our expectations for relationships and marriages are greater than to just, make it "'til death do us part."

With so few maps to measure success or failure, we've consciously or unconsciously adopted business models. Even couples who have never run, operated, or participated in an active business, may be using these skills because they are everywhere in our culture.

We pick up a tabloid, waiting for a dividing bar, as the conveyor belt stalls, and read about the emotional misery of the rich and famous. We try to look nonchalant, but those are the faces of our culture's goals. We struggle to understand how their achievements haven't guaranteed relationship bliss. We're sure, if given the chance, it would be different for us. A roll of antacids moves toward our groceries and we plop a plastic bar down on the conveyor belt and re-rack the paper.

Those who are proficient at business have admired people who make things happen. They have enlisted the closers to their own teams. They have found ways to produce results where others couldn't. Then they are confused when these strategies don't lead to warm and safe feelings with their life partners.

The naturals at business thrive on ambition. At work they're able to fully express their creativity, and feel excitement in their veins. For these few people, their passion *is* the art of business.

I'm not talking about the workaholic who escapes uncomfortable feelings, or the consequences of neglecting other areas of their life through work. I'm talking about people who feel most energized when immersed in the game of business: Those rare few who loved selling cookies, wrapping paper or magazine subscriptions in elementary school; anything, just to experience the impact of making a deal.

If you're one of these talented people, celebrate your skills and natural ability, but if you're curious about another set of skills to create closeness and emotional intimacy in your relationships, they're available. You can learn them. One catch is you may have to start by accepting that some important things are arbitrary. This may be difficult since *arbitrary* and *subjective* are not useful business practices.

In business, nothing should be accepted arbitrarily. Before investing in a new advertising campaign, market research should be done. Before purchasing a new location, competitors should be evaluated. Resumes should be read and references verified before hiring a new employee. Business is about making decisions based on solid facts. Good business practice is to keep the facts in full view at all times.

Life partners of driven people may feel lonely and neglected, especially if the business application is brought home. Claiming that they're "doing all this" for them is unlikely to create a feeling of being special. If the ambitious partner finds their greatest excitement and fulfillment in making money, their companion may begin to feel less and less important. There are ways of addressing this and avenues to start feeling close again.

Sometimes we become so focused on providing the customer with comparative facts, testimonials and scientific proof, that we forget what every child knows coming into the world: *We have an innate right to our internal state. We have every right to our emotions and our wishes.* None of us was born wondering "Do I have enough substantiating evidence to justify my hopes and dreams?"

On some level, we all want to be authentically ourselves, have the one who loves us accept the way we feel in the moment, and acknowledge they've heard our wishes...even the ones that will never come true.

In work environments, practical, related results are important. You can't tell a customer, "I'll have it to you at some date, not really sure when," or "I might have that model in stock. If not, I'll just send you something else." A business needs expedient, *specific* results. An effective business gets these results as efficiently as possible.

To go as fast as possible over an issue in a relationship, is to not have a relationship. It's like replacing a meal at a fine dining restaurant by taking a pill that makes you feel full. You'd miss the experience. The purpose of going to a nice restaurant is for the experience. There's no pageantry or ambiance in a protein drink or an energy bar. Producing the end result makes sense in running a business, but focusing only on the result of a terrific meal is senseless.

Process is what gets left out in a bottom-line agenda. Process is the *quality* of our experience. It is mindfulness of the present. When we focus on a conclusion or result we ignore what we or our partner feels right here and now. We overlook how things are and don't allow ourselves to slow down to be in awe of them. This requires hanging out with uncertainty, and the gnawing angst of waiting. It takes acknowledging our partner's wants and desires, without jumping to the conclusion of whether we can accommodate them or not.

The bonding in relationship happens during self-revealing and vulnerability. These only happen in the present moment while compassionately holding the tension in the middle of not knowing how it will turn out. I will explain this in detail later.

Awareness of our wants and dreams, without demanding they be immediately met, creates a new focus in relationship. This new focus has a power no business model can offer. Being curious about your partner's wants and needs means you're willing to look into the mystery and excitement of who they are. The personal differences in relationships are part of what makes you feel special and accepted for what you bring as an individual to the partnership.

These are the arbitrary aspects of relationship building. You can't spend these disclosures at the grocery store. They don't add to your net worth and they certainly aren't quantifiable when you do attain them. They are, by their nature, ambiguous, and defined differently in each relationship. You can't look up "emotional closeness" in Consumer Reports and find the best brand. Since it's a process, there is no specific finish line.

Your own description of feeling special and close to your partner may even seem fuzzy and indescribable at first. You might find it frustrating to head toward something with no way of ever truly arriving in a concrete sense.

One of the first challenges I see with couples is that many aren't even aware of their wants or feelings. This obviously makes it hard to discuss them. It may not seem like you have any at first, but if you're arguing or debating over an issue, you must have *something* you want (even if it's just having your partner understand or see your perspective).

If you're willing to put energy into fighting about it, you probably also have some feelings about the topic as well (even if they're uncomfortable and hard to define). The concepts in the following chapters will provide specific ways to build emotional closeness in your relationship, with process as the focus, not an outcome.

***

A conversation in the parking lot after a couple's first therapy session:

"That makes no sense. Say it again." He squinted his eyes, trying to squeeze out distraction and only concentrate on who was in front of him.
"There's a difference between telling me what to do and saying what you're feeling."
"It's the way you're saying it that confuses me."
"Sounds like a cop-out to me. I feel like you're not even trying to understand."
"Remember, the therapist said, 'No feeling word ever follows the word like.'"
"Sounds like psychobabble to me."
"You're just throwing up confusion, so you don't have to think about what I'm saying."
"I'm hurt that you'd say that."
"There it is!"
"What?"
"You told me how you feel, instead of what I should be doing!"
"I did?"
"Yes!"
"That's progress?"

14

"It's a start."

Exercises:
Notice when your conversation is focused on getting results or when it conveys real curiosity about your partner.
Take a quiz on temperament (www.PleaseUnderstndMe.com) and read about your and your partner's temperaments.

Examples

Boardroom:
"I'm so busy, I don't have time to go to the bank.
Just drop off the deposit on your way to work."
 "You don't have to make such a big deal out
of it. Just help me out for once!"
"You shouldn't feel that way! They didn't mean anything by it!"

Bedroom:
"I really want to feel in partnership with you.
Are you comfortable with how things are?"
"It's really hard for me to talk about feelings.
I'm not sure I even have the words."

"I feel kind of uncomfortable when that happens. I
wish I had better coping skills for those times."
"I'd guess you'd never feel this way under these
circumstances, but I'd like your support right
now, even if you don't understand."

Written Exercises:
Write a sentence you've said that was focused on getting something done.
Write a sentence where you indicated you were really interested in what your partner wanted or how they felt.

Chapter Two

Better Mouse Traps Franchise
(The History of Business)

This year I made family tree books to give my adult children. With old black and white pictures, handwritten census pages and ink-splotched immigration documents, I tried to paint a picture of their roots. I wanted them to see how much work their ancestors put in so they could have the privilege of their cushy California lifestyle.

Business has always been about creating a supply for a demand. My father's ancestors were astute tenacious farmers. For generations they calculated the terrain and crops that would bring the most profit. Things were far from easy, despite their success. One sepia print showed a Mennonite woman, her black bonnet strings tied at her chin, her drooping abdomen war-scarred from 14 births (only six lived past the age of two), staring down at an open coffin resting on barren ground. Inside, her husband laid on a hand-stitched quilt, decorated with vines and flowers, his ragged hands folded over his chest. They'd left Moloschna after the new Tsar of Russia refused to sell their colony more farming land. They sold their ranch, equipment, livestock and home, piling three small kids into a cart, then a train, a steam ship and another train and headed to Oklahoma. After reading about opportunities and the climate, in California, my great-great-grandparents left caring friends and community celebrations for Escondido. They struggled for twelve years to get a new Mennonite ranch off the ground, with the breaking point coming when they lost another all night battle against the frost. Fought with smudge pots filled with "slop distillate," of crude oil waste, they couldn't keep the frost-bitten oranges from thawing too quickly in the morning sun; the second year in a row of destroyed crops devastating them. As the spoiled oranges dropped from the trees, they sold their orchards and headed to Shafter to start over.

I couldn't run my practice without phones, computers, copiers, email, electric lights and transportation. Many of my clients couldn't participate fully in therapy without medications and interventions that are the results of business innovation. Everything that makes my life easier, safer and more comfortable than my great-great-grandmother's life on the Molotschna River, comes from business.

Obviously, convincing others to exchange valuables or barter for services has been a core human endeavor for thousands of years. When a competitor develops a faster, cheaper product they win customers. When a new development makes a past service obsolete, a new paradigm reigns. We never want to be left behind, trapped with no options, or be seen as weak. Gathering, trading, inventing, marketing, and selling define ambition and advancement, but the Golden Rule of relationships shouldn't be, "The one with the gold, rules."

We've been raised to be defensive. As a kid, if you wanted the new toy in the TV commercial you learned how to have a "good sales pitch." Persuasive evidence got better results than expressing any feeling or revealing your hope of what your friends would say when they saw you with the prized trophy. If we didn't have good enough reasons, we were left feeling shamed, unseen and misunderstood.

We're socialized out of paying attention to our wants and our feelings. Good parenting includes social skills like impulse control (that we don't have the right to *express* our feelings any way we wish) and the value of delayed gratification (we can't *have* everything we wish for).

These are important life-skills, but most of our parents didn't distinguish between our *internal* state and the *external* expression of it, so both got suppressed (or worse) punished. They didn't know any better, so they did the best they could. This common childhood experience sets us up to be defensive when someone tells us we *should* feel differently or *should* want something different. We already assume that we'll have to defend our feelings and support our right to our dreams.

17

Most people have never even heard healthy dialogue, the kind focused on connection and relationship building. They've seen a tension-filled sitcom showing people blaming each other for how they feel, and demanding they get what they want doesn't model good relationship tools; probably not a video game or TV show where characters were self-revealing and taking personal responsibility for their feelings. There wouldn't be enough tension or drama in it.

For many people, their emotions and wants have been so hidden and controlled, they cannot even express them out loud. This is the primary reason partners in a relationship end up feeling invisible and lonely. It's possible through your personal exploration to become aware of your emotions and dreams. It may be scary, vulnerable work, but millions have done it. Be brave, give it a try.

Exercise:
Notice where an outcome-focus conversation is important in your life.

<u>Examples</u>

Boardroom:
"Hurry up we'll be late!"
"Just finish it. It doesn't need to be perfect."
"You have a dozen already; you shouldn't want another one!"

Bedroom:
"That looks tough. How are you doing?"
"Would you like my help or are you doing okay?"
"I'm on overload. I want to take a walk.
Would you like to come, too?"

Written Exercises:
What's your favorite show?
What's the protagonist's goal?
Who in your childhood had difficulty finishing things?
Describe a time that affected you.

Chapter Three

Bringing the Employee Handbook Home

Clients often ask me why their family members have taken to heart what a therapist told them and changed their behaviors. They can't understand why their loved ones never listen to them or take their advice seriously. I understand that it can be confusing, but I encourage people not to take it too personally.

Suggestions from a family member are always complicated. Family cares more, their well-meaning statements have history, insinuations, expectations and an emotional charge. Therapy is more detached. The therapist has no investment in whether or not a client is ready to make changes, or makes those changes slowly or quickly. Because of this lack of attachment, a therapist's encouragement is often seen as more objective, with no ulterior motives.

An employee handbook is also a detached written statement. It's a written statement of the employer's rules for employees. There's no close personal attachment in an employee/employer relationship. It's not an egalitarian conversation. It's a skewed relationship, by design and by agreement.

People at work can be friendly, but there's much less real intimacy in employer/employee conversations. These relationships are not equal. The rules in an employee handbook are directives: "Set the alarm when you close," "Wash your hands after using the restroom," "Leave all cell phones in the lockers," etc.

One of the primary reasons passion and sexual desire goes out of relationships is because one (or both) partners have stopped sharing as equals. Instead of saying, "Sweetie, I'm missing alone time with you. I'd like to go to the movies"—A *feeling* statement and a *want* statement—they're now giving directives: "You need to quit being so busy," "You have to reassess your priorities," "You need to make time for us!"

The biggest problem with directive statements is that they create a skew in the relationship. One person is now talking down to the other as an inferior. Directives are *not* vulnerable statements. They don't reveal your feelings or share your dreams. It's easier to tell someone what they should do than it is to say, "I don't have coping skills for this and I just wanted you to know how sad I am."

Directives are often appropriate in a work setting if there is an understood hierarchy. Upon being hired, an employee is informed that they report to a manager and that manager reports to the supervisor above them. Businesses run better with this kind of structure.

Emotionally close, equal and respectful partners foster intimacy and sexual feelings in their relationship. These are the earmarks of a close loving relationship.

Most HR departments issue mandates forbidding superiors from dating those they manage. These rules are set in place to mitigate abuses of power and any potential emotional fallout. Peers make the best partners. In our culture (all cultures in fact) there's a natural taboo against sexual and feelings between parents and children. Hierarchy naturally squelches true romantic attraction.

You may not mean to talk down to your partner, but if you problem-solve without including them, you may be acting like a boss. By demanding an outcome to your own agenda, you may elicit a defensive response from your partner, even a fake, pretending acquiescence. Even if it's not obvious at the time, you'll find out when there's no follow-through on the agreement. Even if you feel there's a crisis to be averted, one person can't be the "boss" in a relationship. An authoritarian system will fail. (If both parties agree to this hierarchy, as in some traditional cultures where women are still considered property, they are probably not reading this book, anyway.)

Employers and administration are responsible for crisis management. When business takes a downturn, it's important to "get out there and hustle." Businesses that don't take action when trouble is brewing won't be in business long. Specific steps to "turn business around" are imperative. This requires a focus on explicit, measurable outcomes and holding employees accountable for creating these outcomes by a specified time. Employers and managers who can do this are seen as effective, but they are not romantic life partners.

When one partner "knows" what needs to happen, or one person in a relationship "knows" what the other person should *do*, bigger problems are created. "Taking charge" and pointing out what changes have to happen, and by when, puts one partner in a subservient position. Intimacy is unlikely with this emotional skew. Defensiveness, excuses, projections and passivity are more likely when a partner is told how to change.

I often hear women say, "He gives me simplistic answers about what I should do. I feel demeaned and patronized. I just want him to hear me and believe I'm smart enough to figure a way out. I'd like to not feel alone while I'm working it out." The partner, on the other hand, believes that if he gives her a solution, he's being caring and supportive.

Men tend to complain similarly: "She doesn't think I can do anything. She has to micromanage everything I do! Can't she just hang out and not try to control me?" His partner is under the misconception that if no one makes a mistake, everyone will be happy, thinking she's protecting him from experiencing uncomfortable emotions.

Clients ask me if they have to think about how they say things all the time. I tell them that when things are going well in relationships, there's a natural understanding that both partner's feelings and wants are accepted. There's emotional safety. There's no need for defensiveness. (This does not mean accepting all *outward expressions* of feelings and the right to get everything *you* want, just an unconditional acceptance of each other's internal state.)

When difficult times show up in relationships, these safe assumptions can mysteriously vanish. In fact, if things are really bad, there's a forgoing assumption that partners *will* attempt to disqualify each other's subjective vulnerable disclosures.

In business, if an employee disobeys a rule in the handbook they may be written up with a threat that their job is in jeopardy. This tactic, if used in a marriage or life partnership, is one of the most destructive interactions a relationship can face. A threat to quit the partnership disrupts vulnerability faster than anything else. The relationship is then based in fear. A partner may stop sharing how they really feel or what they really want because they now know that the other partner can "go there.".

Threatening, "I'll take my business elsewhere," or "I have another distributor that will meet my requests," or even knowing you have another job lined up, may all be productive ways of increasing your power in business. However, these strategies annihilate the ability to be intimate and emotionally safe in a relationship.

Once abandonment is threatened a partner is now faced with the choice of withdrawing their openness from the relationship, or leaving it all together. If their choice is to stay, but hide their vulnerable feelings and wants, the beginning of a sad, lonely, invisible journey has begun. If the partner decides that self-expression and being seen is more important, then the relationship may be over. Ultimatums, however practical in business, are no way to conduct a healthy intimate relationship.

If this is a habit you or your partner has, there is a way out: First, you must acknowledge to yourself that you couldn't think of any other way to express your frustration, anger, sadness, loneliness, disappointment, fear, etc. Forgive yourself for putting the destructive ultimatums into your relationship, and begin making a serious effort to collect or create other ways of expressing uncomfortable feelings. (Journaling can help.)

Develop a vocabulary so you can say, "I feel angry and what I really want is for you to know how mad I am," or "I feel alone and depressed and I notice I'm wanting you to take care of me," or "I'm fighting the urge to tell you how to run your life, and it's taking all the willpower I can generate, I'm afraid something bad will happen to you, and I don't want that."

When you have words to express your internal state you can approach your partner and let him or her know that you feel bad about using threats and extortion to express your discomfort. Let him or her know you're committed to not using hostage language any more, and that you're open to hearing how he or she feels about your past threats.

It's important to keep the invitation open. When someone is scared (which is what happens when someone is threatened) he or she may be reluctant for a while to say out loud how they feel and what they want. Be patient. Demonstrate you're not going to keep using direct threats or insinuations.

Don't be surprised if, when you have shown you are open to hearing how they feel, the flood gates open. Try to think of this as a gift. If you revert back to giving evidence and facts to get them to "calm down," you'll very likely make things worse. If you can stay present, putting your own agenda aside so that your partner's feelings and wants can be acknowledged, you may be surprised at what they really want. Many times, after expressing hurt and fear, a partner just wants to be held or reassured of your commitment level.

As a final note in this chapter, there may be a few people who are not interested in having an emotionally close relationship in their life. That must be accepted. A close intimate relationship, where two people feel emotionally safe and in a life partnership, is not everyone's goal.

It's important that you're honest with yourself and give your partner the opportunity to be honest as well. This isn't a popular question.

Ask about this before you decide to do the work it takes to create an intimate relationship. It's all right to choose no relationship or a different kind of relationship, but a close emotional partnership, based on mutual respect and vulnerability, is a process-based adventure. It can be a wild ride and it has no set handbook.

The Employee Handbook Says:

1) Take your scheduled breaks in the designated areas.
2) Give 24-hour notice if you're going to be late for work due to doctor's appointment.
3) No personal calls at the office.
4) Computer activity is monitored.
5) Clean up the break area before you return to work.
6) You must comply with random drug tests.
7) You will be sent home if dressed inappropriately.
8) Assessments will only be given at annual reviews.
9) After three written notices you will be dismissed.
10) Offensive language will not be tolerated.

Exercise:
Observe the areas of your relationship where one of you tries to be the boss.

Examples

Boardroom:
"If it's that much trouble, quit already!"
"When was the last time you cleaned up the kitchen?
"Did you clean out the garage like you said you were going to?"
"If you just set up a plan (schedule, outline, list, etc.) you'd be able to get it all done, and not feel overwhelmed!"

Bedroom:
"I wish you'd tell me how you're feeling. I care about you."
"I'm here for you. I don't want you to feel like you're in this alone."
"You seem overwhelmed. Do you want to talk about it?"

"I'm scared when you talk like that. What is it
that you'd like me to really understand?"

Written Exercises:
Write about a time when one of you made
a threat in your relationship.
What would you like to tell your partner about that?

Chapter Four

A Good Resume isn't Worth a Byte

There are many things we can conclude from researching the past. Some of these turn out to be accurate and some do not.

I treated a lot of shocked and depressed business owners during the Great Recession of 2008 and in the fallout through the next few years. These highly successful people were devastated by the chaos and loss of control. Grieving owners had to let employees go even though they knew there were no other jobs available. Owners closed satellite stores then downsized to one and eventually worked from home. They tearfully sold vacation homes, and then their primary residences. And many, because they had gone in debt to meet payroll, had such bad credit they couldn't even qualify to rent an apartment. Many reluctantly went through assets designated for children's college tuition just to keep food on the table.

I witnessed creative people who brought new products, entertainment, technology and delivery methods to Orange County, the U.S. and the world, be thrown back to square one. They couldn't depend on the tried and true adjustments of the past. They didn't have the lines of credit to fall back on. They were at a loss to figure out their next move.

A few said they saw the bubble coming, but didn't know what else they could do. A few said they knew the financial collapse was inevitable, but were hit with health issues or divorces and had no way to financially prepare. Most believed they could ride it out. A few did.

Studying the economy and the history of international finance may give one insights and the ability to predict some of the ebb and flow of business. The past can shed some light on the present when it comes to the economy.

Being familiar with the history of one's industry can buy some calculated projections. Collecting a complete background is also helpful in hiring reliable employees, so it's understandable that many people mistakenly bring a résumé when choosing personal relationships.

There are several problems with this. The first is, that human beings are not walking redundancies, merely sums of their past. We're not computers that spit out the same data that's been input. We're not broken machines that keep making the same errors over and over. We're alive, dynamic, humans with genius in every one of us that can redefine situations, recontextualize events, and apply new information to situations. Human beings, when not afraid, are capable of generating infinite alternatives.

As Dr. Wayne Dyer said, "The wake of a boat doesn't affect its course..." The past is not what's in charge: It's the person at the helm of his or her life. No matter where the boat has been, the ripples in the water behind it (which are an accurate indicator of where it was) have no power to control the boat's direction.

When an employer is looking for a new employee one of the most important places to start is their CV. Checking with past employers and verifying personal references are imperatives to hiring good help. History gathering is important to bring productive help into your business.

You can't collect enough historical data to decide if a person is a good partner for you. You can't avoid future fights that start with "You're just like your mother/father!" by interviewing the family. You can't tell if you'll be inspired by a person by finding out how many people they dated.

I'm often asked by business-focused clients, "What's the most important information to collect when looking for a mate?" I tell them, "It's much more complicated than evaluating potential employees."

Objective fact finding may be interesting, but you can see this checklist may not be asking the right questions:

My Checklist *(Check all that apply)*

☐ *Do your parents (and by extension, YOU) have money?*
☐ *Can you support me in the manner to which I am accustomed?*
☐ *Do you look good on my arm?*
☐ *I'm smarter than you, right?*

One of the things that makes this task so complex is that employers can verify information on a job application. There are objective sources to check to determine if a particular applicant has increased revenue in their last career position.

As all researchers know, self-report can be quite subjective. We talk about the aspects of our personality we think are most important and the ones we're proudest of. We all also have psychological blind spots. Much of what motivates us (and that we react to) is unconscious or hidden by our defense mechanisms. People are built with these defenses to keep stressful facts off our minds, and for very good reasons: If every memory of our past was on the surface and interrupting our every thought, we wouldn't be able to carry on a conversation.

If we were remembering every bad thing that happened to us in grade school, how we felt when our pets died, how we felt at graduations, birthday parties, holidays, funerals, etc., and vivid memories of everything we'd ever done, seen, smelled, tasted, heard, etc., flooded our minds, how on earth would any of us ever have a clear thought, much less function in society!?

When you ask a potential partner about their past, many painful events, memories and feelings are buried or glossed over (due either to resolving them, or possibly due to *not* having resolved them). Even if they could describe significant life-changing events, you're still hearing and interpreting these through your own history, *your* blind spots and own assumptions about life.

There is very little objectivity in self-report, other than to find out what people themselves believe is important on a conscious level. There is even less objectivity in evaluating this information in a new relationship. There are variables: like physical attractiveness, what your friends said about him/her, how long you've been pining over this person, your last relationship issues and how this person compares to them, financial issues, your family's preferences, your childhood images of who you would end up with---the list is endless and extremely subjective, if even conscious.

In a work setting, a person is hired to do a particular job. Even if that person isn't someone you'd want to sit around and chat with some evening, you may still find them the "perfect person for the job." Most employers hire based on how they predict an employee will function in a work environment (or in their sales territory or cocooning from home) about 8-10 hours a day. In a personal relationship, there will be many different settings, many different stresses, and days where you're together 24 hours a day, sometimes seven days a week.

In a life partnership, most people want to be accepted for who they really are. Not accepted just because of what they can do for someone else. Home life shouldn't be a performance like a job. In fact, when work stress takes its toll, having a loved one provides a safe haven to come home to. Hard working people crave a sanctuary where they're given the benefit of the doubt and can lick their wounds from the day's stresses.

Whether someone comes from the "right" background, has the "right" letters after their name, or makes a "good" living, may tell you nothing about their ability to be fully present and accepting in your relationship.

If a new date blames the ending of their last relationships on the absent party, ask a ton of questions. If you're dating someone who blames the demise of all their past relationships on all their old partners, you're likely to be the next partner to be blamed for their problems. On the other hand, if a new date owns their share of the issues in their past relationships, can talk about the ways they've grown as a person, and are able to take future responsibility for their feelings and wants, then they may have something special to bring to a relationship with you.

- Listen for their ability to talk about internal states (emotions and desires), not just outward accomplishments.
- Listen for insinuations that if you say "no," it will always

be an accepted and respected answer. (Pressuring you to change your "no" to a "yes" would be the opposite of this.)

- Listen for when they take personal responsibility for their own feelings or if they blame someone else.
- Listen for gratitude and comments about where they feel blessed in life. Someone who is always looking at how things can be improved upon, may be good at making new products to sell, but will wear thin quickly as an intimate partner.
- Listen for expansive, over-inclusive conversations, ones heavily burdened down by evidence, and lacking vulnerability. This may be entertaining at first, but will soon come to sound like a long-winded sales pitch, aimed at you.
- Listen for their verbal validations of your own feelings and wishes. (Telling you that you're "overreacting" or "don't have a good enough reason" would be the opposite of this.)
- Look for their ability to validate your uncomfortable feelings without trying to change them. (Acknowledging your discomfort doesn't mean they take responsibility for it. We are always responsible for our own feelings.)
- Look for their skill at endorsing your dreams, without evaluating the probability of them happening.
- Listen for their own disclosure of feelings. (Remember no *real* feeling follows the words, "like" or "that.". "I feel that you take too long," is *not* a feeling. "I feel frustrated," is.)
- Listen for their participation in activities that give back to the world, and make it a better place.
- Listen for their participation in activities that better themselves: classes, athletics, self-help groups, and spiritual or educational pursuits.
- Listen for that endearing characteristic of curiosity, without judgment: the ability to be in awe of mysteries that may never be conclusively solved. (Sustained romantic love always has some of this quality.)
- Watch how they treat other people. That is how they will eventually treat you.

When dating, be open to hearing all feelings and wants. If you are subtly preferring only comfortable feelings or start asking for substantiation for uncomfortable ones ("Why are you so unhappy?"), you may not get an accurate picture. Show up without judgment and an attachment to how this person *should* be. Ask yourself if you have real listening to bring to a relationship.

Know what your dreams and goals are in your life *before* you connect with a life partner. Know first where you are going, and *then* with whom. If you get this order reversed, you will be looking for someone else to give their life meaning and purpose. One person can *never* give this to another; it is a gift we can only give ourselves. Bringing a fully developed adult---one who knows what they want and how they feel--- is the greatest gift one can give to a relationship. Only then can you not make your partner responsible for your happiness and greater meaning in life; and that is essential to be able to stay close and connected when there's emotional pain.

By knowing *where* you are going, you've found your own purpose in life. You believe you are here to make a difference. Your work brings you fulfillment. If your job doesn't have intrinsic being of service or fulfillment in it, where else can you volunteer, mentor, or guide others? Where do you give back? How is your presence on the planet making a difference? How do you feel connected to a bigger whole?

If you do not have answers to these questions, seek them out! It's impossible to go into a relationship without knowing these answers and not place an undue burden on it.

This does not mean you need to take a month or a year off to volunteer services in a disadvantaged country. It means that you take responsibility for finding meaning in your own life. It means understanding that your life is bigger than just having your own wants and needs met.

I've met hundreds of financially secure people in long-term relationships, who, from an outsider's view, would seem to have it all, that are miserable and feel lonely. This depression and anxiety comes from expecting that something outside themselves is going to bring them peace and contentment. This is never the case. Situations reveal us, they don't make us. More about that later.

Focusing on what a significant other can add to your life will always create disappointment. In business a great employee must work toward the goals of the company. In personal relationships, a great partner is one that you find you are the best version of yourself with. This may have little or nothing with what they *do*, and everything to do with who they *are*.

Exercise:

Pay attention to what you think makes you a "good catch."

Examples

Boardroom:

"How many years of education do you have?"
"How much money do you make?"

"What have you done for me lately?"

Bedroom:

"I am so glad I can come home and relax with you."
"I love watching you light up when you talk about your volunteer project."
"I feel so rejuvenated and put back together when we spend alone time together."

Written Exercises:

What do you have a passion for outside your relationship?
What dreams for your future have you invested in?
Write a paragraph describing how you are committed to keeping yourself enthusiastic about life and your plans for personal growth over the next 15 years.

Chapter Five

Selling Only Makes Sales

I grew up with conflicting messages about selling. At six, I was given a fish bowl with a couple of guppies by a neighbor that was moving away. After about a week, I noticed a glob of eggs floating around the plastic greenery. To my delight, my mother informed me they would hatch, but I would have to make sure the parents didn't eat the babies. So I carefully set up a mayonnaise jar nursery and moved all the hatching specks to safety with a spoon. I rubbed dry smelly flakes between my fingers into a powder to feed the darting little tykes. When they were big enough to distinguish their gender I put a male and a female each in sandwich bags filled with water and secured them with twist ties. I put the live water balloons in my wagon and set out to make my fortune around the block.

At five cents a bag, I felt successful returning home with an empty wagon and jingling coins in my pink purse. As I spread my earnings on the kitchen table, my mother informed me in a dire voice that she'd found that the *Encyclopaedia Britannica* gave many different scientific names for my little swimmers. I beamed and sat up a little straighter. I sold *exotic* pets to my friends and neighbors.

"No," my mother said, "You profited from the sin of amalgamation. Guppies could only have bred by Satan's work. They're not the same as the fish at the time of the flood." I frowned. This wasn't going well. "And because you've sinned by breeding those abominations in my home you must give the money to a Sabbath School Investment Project." So my guppy adventure ended with her church friends shaking her hand and congratulating her on her daughter's moment at the pulpit, telling about the Guppy Investment Project for the missionaries.

Not all sales for the church were tangible. Some were long term investments. In my house, Saturday afternoons were dedicated to entertaining potential new converts. This was a time to sell them on our religion, especially the in-house bible studies. Who wouldn't want to know about the Time of Trouble where fourth commandment keepers would be hunted down and killed? Or the addictive danger of vinegar in salad dressing? Or the deformities in children caused by masturbation? Knowing the exact second of sundown on Friday night could keep one from sinning and burning up with the wicked at the end of the world? It was better than the Ginsu knife sales show at the fair! My father welcomed the Mormon missionaries, the Jehovah's Witnesses, even the Helms Bakery delivery man in for debate.

My skills at convincing still serve me well, however I leave them at the office, the TV studio and the lecture stage. The man of my life isn't interested in being convinced. He wants to laugh and imagine with me. We couldn't create the humor and aliveness we do if we were stuck trying to sell each other on our point of view.

I admit we're bombarded with mailboxes full of ads, social media product placement, billboards while we drive, commercials before we watch movies, and pop-ups chosen by cookies while we try to read the news. It seems everywhere we turn someone is focused on "selling" or convincing someone else about an idea or product.

We don't have to work very hard to adapt a sales patter. The conversations are everywhere, so most of us have picked them up without even noticing. We communicate to our loved ones with a sales tone, focusing on how things could be "better." Sales conversations are about giving good reasons for changing and improving things.

In everyday life, most of us hate to be bothered by sales calls, yet many partners don't hesitate to use these tools in their homes. The more evidence, facts, history and comparisons to others that are included, the more like sales a conversation feels. The faster and the harder the evidence flies, the less likely the targeted person will have a good comeback. And if they don't have a good response, then they are much more likely to appear to agree with the convincing salesperson. If we can get away, we usually classify these pushy people as unsafe and react to protect ourselves.

There's a high price to pay for using sales communication in your intimate relationship. Most couples are shocked when they have to pay it. The price is the loss of closeness and intimacy. This natural loss of passion and emotional connection when a partner tries to defend off the pressuring partner may surprise couples who believe they've been fighting to get these things all along.

Emotional self-protection means staying connected to who we are as individuals. On a deep level, we all know we feel what we feel and want the things we dream of, even if the evidence indicates that others would feel or wish for different things. Both individuals retaining their dignity, their unique sense of individuality, are primary components of healthy relationships. If one partner hard sells the other on how they ought to feel and what they should want, there's only *one* vital person in the relationship. The other is a shell of a person, mirroring only what they are sold. Both partners will feel lonely and unloved if this happens. Innately, we all know this, and that's why, even if unconsciously, the wall goes up when we feel barraged by "sales talk" aimed at changing our internal state.

Here is an example of how a sales dialogue can sabotage problem-solving:

Raymond: "I had Italian for lunch. Pick somewhere else."
Pat: "You *said* we'd go to Roma's tonight.
You change your mind every time."
Raymond: "Calm down, you're over-reacting. It's just dinner."
Pat: "Calm down!? That's you're answer
when you don't care what I want?"
Raymond: "Stop thinking in absolutes. You
have no idea what kind of day I've had!"
Pat: "Someone has to care about absolutes. You
change your mind like you change your clothes!"

Raymond: "Great. So now *I'm* unstable. You're
the one who personalizes everything. I've about
had it with you being so unreasonable."
Pat: "You don't know how I feel and you don't care. It's your
way or the highway. We'll go wherever you want---again."

Even if one of them sells the other on a resolution---they pick an
outcome and end up at a restaurant---there's a low chance they'll
enjoy the meal together and probably feel even more distant
afterwards.

April: "I read really bad reviews on that dinner
place. Can't we go somewhere else?"
Sam: "But I've got a gift card for it. Let's just try it."
April: "You could take a client there. It really
doesn't sound that good to me."
Sam: "You really don't want to go, do you? I
don't want you to feel pressured. What did the bad
review say that bothered you so much?"
April: "Well, their special is that stupid dish my stepdad always
made us eat."
Sam: "I remember you telling me about that. Ugggg."
April: "The review wasn't really all *that* bad.
I just wanted to focus on us tonight."
Sam: "Wow, I'm glad you could share that
with me. It's important to me."
April: "Thanks. He really was a jerk. Let's
just go get something to eat."

April and Sam let go of the sales conversation and talked about
feelings and wants, rather than providing evidence why each
should get their own way. Whatever restaurant they end up at,
there's a very good chance they'll enjoy the meal and their time
together and feel closer afterwards.

Exercise:
Pay attention when you're using facts and evidence to sell your
partner on something.

Examples

Boardroom:

"See? Yelp voters agree with me!"
"I know you'll like this one better."
"If you'd just done it my way, you wouldn't
have this consequence!"

Bedroom:

"Before we decide anything, I really want
to know how you feel about it."
"I feel pretty strongly about this, but I don't want
you to feel resentful or invisible." "You seem a little
defensive. Is this reminding you of anything else?"

Written Exercises:

Write a paragraph describing something you've tried
to "sell" your partner on in the last few days.
Write another paragraph, using your own words, to describe
your "feelings" and "wants" about this topic. Focus on
being vulnerable and sharing things that may be hard to
reveal, rather than getting the outcome you want. (This
exercise can be done verbally as well with your partner.)

Chapter Six

Destroying Relationships with Skills that Build Business

Aristotle Onassis once said, "The secret of business is to know something that nobody else knows." In relationships, however, secrets divide and transparency creates trust and connection.

This is one example of how maps are only good for the territory they're intended for. Just because a set of skills may have worked in one place, doesn't mean they'll work everywhere, but it's hard to learn new strategies. Most of us have worked hard at developing the ones we already have. We need good reasons and some hope we'll be able to attain the skills in order to focus that much energy on something new and difficult.

When Samuel Chapin, my earliest American ancestor on my mother's side, shook off his sea legs around 1635, and analyzed what could be profitable in a wilderness that looked nothing like Dartmouth, England, he knew he needed a new set of skills. In Roxbury, he learned the colonies were more like theocracies than extensions of England, so Samuel immediately joined a Puritan church to enjoy "freeman" privileges, including land ownership, voting, and most importantly for him, governing others for a profit. In the colonies, salaries were more often paid with land, crops, silk, buttons, rum, wine, sugar and livestock than the silver crowns and sovereigns back home. He saw opportunity in the new system where others only saw depravation.

In 1642, he arrived ready to trade governance for land and wages in the raw territory that his friend, William Pynchon, had bought from the Indians with 18 hoes, 18 fathoms of wampum, 18 coats, 18 hatchets and 18 knives. Adhering to this new form of law, Samuel became the first deacon in Springfield, Massachusetts. He was included in a 1645 commission that divided the town up into equal lots. He was then on the first Selectman committee, where he settled disputes, admitted inhabitants to the township, regulated highways, fences, finances and religious adherence, like not profaning, kissing, or missing church. He presided over violations of laws concerning romantic passion, business, and religion, which encompassed both: no PDA or shops open on the Sabbath. This same year, he became the town Constable and was certified to hand down any sentence less than death, loss of a limb or banishment. A humiliating afternoon in the stocks, or a neck-stretching pillory with one's ears nailed to the wood, public floggings, brandings, tongue piercings, years in shackles as a slave, or being pulled behind a boat, were all still at his disposal.

In 1648, Magistrate William Pynchon was labeled a heretic for writing a book that challenged the idea that only the clergy could interpret scripture and also the predetermination ideas of Calvinistic doctrine. After a public book burning, William, Henry Smith and the minister, Mr. Moxon were removed from their official positions. William's son and son-in-law replaced the heretics' official positions---along with Deacon Samuel Chapin. Someone arranged to have a well-publicized witch trial of Mr. Parson and his wife scheduled the same day as Pynchon's. The distraction probably allowed Pynchon, his son, and the minister to return to England alive. The witches were found guilty and Mr. Parson fled the county, leaving his wife to die in prison.

New times required new applied skills. As for the history of human experience, expecting romantic love in marriage is a relatively new concept. Most of our distant ancestors viewed marriage as a financial or religious commitment. Women, for the most part, were property and weddings were arranged based on this assumption. Now we're raised with stories of love and connectedness, so we've come to believe that loving relationships do exist, even if we've never personally seen that New World.

I see couples in my office struggle to find ways of talking about this romantic connection. Often they'll try to harness that loving feeling by comparing who does more for the other one, as if being productive could somehow create real intimacy.

Rating productivity is a business model, however, it *can't* be the criterion for a healthy relationship. On some level, we're all familiar with this idea. Marriage vows usually include some form of, "for richer, for poorer, and in sickness and in health." These are commitments to be loving and accepting, specific promises *not* to evaluate the marriage based on productivity.

We all know people who are extremely industrious in an area or two of their lives: They wear designer clothes, drive a fast car, live with a view, have paid help, tip their hairstylist what we'd spend for dinner, and only find a random valet stub as car clutter, but this person might never be someone we'd trust with our embarrassing secrets or feel safe being emotionally close to.

In business, there's generally a written contract outlining expectations and parameters for employees, franchisees or independent contractors. This keeps the rules consistent and expectations clear for continued employment, suspensions and dismissals. An employer may choose an employee who is useful in the work place but one he/she would never consider spending close personal time with.

Personal intimate relationships are different. Much of what a couple will face over the decades together cannot be outlined contractually. The ups and downs of life's challenges have to be ridden out together, even the ones with no immediate answers. It's important for couples to talk about this struggle. Even when things are not going smoothly or there are hurt feelings, vulnerable personal disclosure creates the opportunity to build closeness and intimacy.

This requires compassion and patience by the partner who may find process conversation less difficult, and it requires self-compassion and courage on the part of the partner who naturally thinks more in terms of outcome.

Be willing to make mistakes. Be willing to be misunderstood, but most of all, be willing to be *seen*. If your goal is to remain invisible and protected by only discussing topics that can be quantified, counted and verified, you will have never create closeness. Protection leads to loneliness. You can never get someone to *do* enough for you to feel loved. You can never feel more loved than you love yourself. You can only feel loved by a partner when you believe you are cherished for who you are, in spite of what you do. In a marriage or life-partner relationship, wielding power over the other will only create resentment and pain.

Some of these power-wielding weapons may be money, or threatening to tell an embarrassing secret to get them on one's side, withholding sex, sharing inappropriate information about the other parent to children, threatening to leave the relationship, silence, not sharing where one has been, or bringing up mistakes of the past.

The power plays come into effect when being right and getting the other person to do what you want them to do is more important than intimacy or having a romantic partner. Many times couples give up and figure, "Well I can't have closeness *and* partnership, so I might as well get him/her to do what I want them to do. Then I won't feel like I'm in this relationship all alone."

The problem with this resignation, is that you'll never know if your partner is capable of connection and intimacy if you believe they can't and don't even try to reach out. If you're sure the only way your partner will do anything respectful to you is if you force it, and "pull your power card," then you'll never know if intimacy is available or not. It's also disrespectful of yourself to not believe you can be loved and respected without force.

The other part of this is that when we force people to do the "right thing" for us, we end up feeling lonely and isolated, anyway. Even if you get your partner to take you to the movies, buy the new house, let you go out to girl's' night out, or fishing with the guys, if you used power over them to make this happen, you've created more pain and distance in the relationship. This is how invisible resentment grows without anything being said.

People are resourceful, and humans have a long history of being able to find out where someone else's weak spot is and use it to make things happen. This tactic may have fewer (but probably some) repercussions in the business world, but in relationships, the repercussions are not only more devastating, they're cumulative. The more often you make something happen by threatening your power over your loved one, the more likely you'll create irreparable damage in your relationship.

It's important to be aware of what you and your partner see as power in your relationship. Just because you wouldn't be threatened by him/her holding a particular thing over your head, doesn't mean it wouldn't be devastating to your loved one.

Demanding that your partner do what you say makes them a subordinate. Blaming them for how you feel makes them responsible for something they can't do anything about. These build hostility. A safe home environment is where partners express their feelings as their own, and share their wants, while being very clear these are not demands.

Exercise:
Find one topic in your relationship you feel is so important you justify becoming "the boss."

Examples

Boardroom:

"This is your job. I do my job, you should do yours!"
"It's obvious you don't think about consequences! When will you ever learn?"
"Can you give me one piece of evidence that shows what you're saying is true?"
"I'm canceling your ATM card and all our credit cards. You have got to learn one of these days."
Bedroom:

"I'm concerned if I try to talk to you, you'll tell
me I'm 'doing it all wrong.' What I'd like is
your acknowledgement that I'm trying."
"When I see you're frustrated and unhappy, I want
to tell you what to do to feel better. What I'd like
is for you to tell me you can handle it."
"I want us to be partners. Sometimes when we do things so
differently, I get scared we won't be on the same page."

Written Exercises:

Write a paragraph describing something that comes easily to you,
but that your partner struggles with.
Write a paragraph describing something that comes more easily
to your partner that you.
Write a list of acknowledgements and compliments you could
give your partner about the things that seem so easy for him/her.
Write a list of ways you have power (or at the beginning of the
relationship had power) in your relationship.
Write a list of ways your partner has (or had) power in your
relationship.
Write a paragraph of ways you used to (or now) react when
someone tries to have power over you.
Write a paragraph about the differences you see in someone
having power over you and in your personal empowerment.
What are the aces you pull out to be sure to get your
partner to do things your way? Write a paragraph of
different ways you would better like to handle this.

Chapter Seven

Everyone Loses in Zero-Sum Games

"When you are content to be simply yourself and don't compare or compete, everybody will respect you." Lao Tzu

When being right is more important than being close, a zero-sum game is being played. When a zero-sum game is played long enough, the protective walls that each partner puts up eventually isolates and separates, making intimacy and closeness impossible.

When I was in junior high school, a substitute teacher wanted to teach our class a lesson by having us play a game. The religious school frowned on competition of any kind and only a temporary teacher would have gotten away with this. The goal, as he told us, was to get as many points as possible, but the caveat was if one team scored a point, the other team automatically lost a point, so the sum of the scores from both sides was always zero.

There was a bright boy in the class who caught on to the object of the game more quickly than the rest of us. He made a deal that looked like it would give everyone a small number of points, but at the last minute he turned the tables and his team got all the points. Our team could see how to get the points back, but we'd been trained not to think this way.

What stands out in my mind about this game, almost 30 years later, is how my classmates and I felt. It was a small school and most of us had been together in the same class since we began attending school. This was the first time we'd been instructed to one-up our peers. It made a lasting impression on me that zero-sum games do more than just have a winner and a loser, they also create a trapped, emotional humiliation for the loser.

Many of the abusive relationships I see in my office are driven by zero-sum games: Each partner has to make the other one wrong in order to be right themselves. Each partner is surprised that over time they have ceased to be as productive as they could be, their sense of self-worth has deteriorated, and hatred and anger at the world has become a way of life.

Current business trainings even encourage teams to stay clear of zero-sum strategies in favor of win/win solutions, but many business conversations are still influenced by this mindset. "What percentage of the market do we have?" insinuates there is only *so* much market! If the assumption is a finite customer base, some other businesses must take a hit if you are to do well.

In a relationship, zero-sum games can become very addicting. Each partner fears that he or she may be humiliated, run over, or controlled if he or she allows the other partner to "win." The increased lack of trust keeps the zero-sum field compelling.

An exercise that can go a long way toward addressing an all or none way of talking is to rate things on a scale of 1-10. This may sound clinical or devoid of feelings, but it can actually help create more closeness. For instance, if one partner says, "You're late again! I'm just never going to make any more plans."

As you can see, all-or-none statements quickly shut down productive communication and put a partner on the defensive. Changing the communication to include the sharing of feelings and wants, and rating these in order of intensity, can be a way to begin self-disclosing.
Example: "I'm really sad about being late when we go places. I'm embarrassed and frustrated. On a scale of one to ten, my frustration is an 8. What I'd like is for us as partners to talk about this. On a scale of 1-10, how big of an issue do you think arriving late is?"

To be the first one to risk and be disclosing can be terrifying. To be the vulnerable one and share something that might be held over your heard takes courage. To stay compassionate and not get defensive takes focus. To remember you're only responsible for your own feelings takes emotional strength. To not buy in to a long-standing zero-sum game in a relationship can take real grit. Be patient with yourself. If you fall back into the game, step back out as quickly as you can. It will make a difference.

Exercise:
What is one topic you believe pits you and your partner against each other?

Examples

Boardroom:

"You think we're going to have sex after you did that?!"
"If you do that again, I'm going to tell
the kids what you're up to!"
"OK, fine, I won't speak to you, either."
"If you just picked up your stuff around
here, I would be nicer to you."
"If you don't do this, don't expect anything else from me!"

Bedroom:

"I'm devastated. I don't know what to do. I feel like retaliating. I'm very angry."
"I'm feeling really distant from you. Could you please tell me a scale of 1-10, how committed are you to the relationship?"
"It's hard for me not to feel like I should rescue you. I want you to be happy. I know when things go wrong you can handle it. I'd just like to be included."
"I want to work on this relationship. I'm hopeful about working this out."

Written Exercises:

Write about the last zero-sum game you found yourself

participating in.

Write about what you were afraid would happen if you "backed down" or showed compassion.

Write about what led to an all or nothing discussion about the topic.

Write a paragraph describing a way to incorporate both of your ideas and short circuit the adversarial stance between the two of you.

If this solution was adopted, what else would you need to get back to feeling special and important to your partner?

Chapter Eight

The Market Value of Your Relationship

"The best and most beautiful things in the world cannot be seen or even touched, They must be felt with the heart." Helen Keller

Deciding the value of a business is an objective process, usually done by means of an appraisal.

In 1880, my great-great-great-grandfather, Edward Olive, was keeping the books for a printing company at age 20. In 1899, he and his business partner, William Myers, had a dream that required financial analysis and the ability to project an establishment's income potential. They pooled money they'd saved from their original company, Olive & Myers, in Indianola, Iowa, a business that did everything from manufacturing furniture, sewing machines and pianos to providing mortuary services. (My great-grandmother told me stories of playing with her sister in the back of the big black horse-drawn hearse.) Together, they appraised eleven different locations west of the Mississippi and calculated the value and projected growth of each business opportunity, finally deciding on a small spring-bed mattress factory in Dallas, Texas. As this first plant grew, they assessed two more factories in Huston, adding these to the first plant to create something bigger and more productive than they could have created back in Iowa.
My great-great-grandfather kept his eyes on the finances as secretary of Myers Olive Manufacturing until he died. He was good at accounting and the business thrived with his skills.

Accounting skills, unlike relationship skills can be totaled at the end of the day to see if there is a profit or a loss. In business, the bottom line is what's carried over to the next month's spreadsheet. In relationships, it's how the interactions are conducted each day that add up, not the conclusions or solutions.

There are many ways to appraise the value of a business. There are companies that specialize in forensic appraisals for dissolutions and commercial brokers. Sometimes, with new technology, price is established through projected sales numbers rather than a confirmed financial history.

Appraising a relationship is a very different process. In fact, we're suspicious if a person talks about their relationship in terms of outcome. Statements like "She has a great trust fund," or "His family name opens doors," make us cringe.

I hear clients evaluate new relationships in many ways: "She's so exciting," "I feel alive when I'm with him," "The world stops when we're together," "I can be myself around him," "We have so much fun together," "We enjoy just hanging out together," "We want the same things in life," "She makes me happy." All these statements are subjective, difficult to quantify and might change from day to day or even minute to minute.

If you Google "How to write a personal ad for a long-term relationship," you'll finds hundreds of books, articles, and links with examples of what makes a "good catch." There's a blog for dating chat abbreviations so you can get the most for your maximum characters in an ad. There are sites to analyze and critique whether the writer of other ads is really a "good catch." There are green links to magazines where you can submit your ad. Matchmaking is a multi-million-dollar industry. Speed dating is alive and well.

Chemistry is not enough to build a lifetime relationship on, but few people are willing to go into a life partnership without at least some of it. Many theories have been written about romantic love, from Plato's souls separated before birth trying to find their missing half, to more cynical psychological theories that we are attracted to what we have lacking in ourselves, to theories that we're born with little maps which are culturally enhanced throughout childhood. We match up prospects against this map and the closer the match, the more we are attracted to the person.

There are qualities of love that defy explanation to friends and family. There's chemistry. There's personal ideals brought with us from childhood. There's, "opposites attract," and there's "having lots in common." There's what your mother thinks is good for you, or what your friends think you need, and the relationship qualities you've vowed never to do without, again. There are many ways to evaluate a relationship, but the worst is using the criteria for valuing a business.

When it comes right down to it, it's impossible to appraise a relationship (new or long-term) with the same objective, quantifiable criteria as one can for appraising a commercial enterprise. It's impossible to evaluate a relationship with theories about the unconscious mind.

All that said, couples and individuals that I see in my practice believe they know whether they are happy or not in their relationship. They know it isn't about productivity. Happy and miserable couples can be productive. They know it's not about net worth. Wealthy people may be lonely or very happy in their relationships. They know it's not about lineage. All sorts of couples have kids. They can tell if they're happy based on their own feelings and experiences.

Happy couples tell me they are best friends or life partners. They describe their relationship as emotionally safe and fun. They enjoy each other's company and look forward to time together. They believe they can say whatever they're feeling and it's emotionally safe to share their dreams, without fear of criticism or belittlement from their partner. They look forward to their partner's support during difficult times. They are excited about sharing and celebrating their successes together. The connection provides a buffer from the challenges of life, and they cherish that.

Most couples who feel this way, don't talk about this outside therapy. Friends and family hear them talk about their kids, their last trip, the sporting event they went to, and the last large purchase they made. That is socially acceptable communication. Most couples talk about their relationship in concrete terms. It's about accomplishments; what they're doing and how productive they are. It's impossible to tell from this kind of conversation how happy or content a couple is.

They're speaking in business terms. They're talking about the bottom line. There is a perception that situations cause our feelings, such as, "Well, if *I* just got back from the Bahamas, *I'd* be happy with my spouse." But this is still an interpretation, and it's very likely that going *anywhere* with a partner you're feeling resentful of, would be another version of misery.

I see scores of individuals who are sad, discouraged, lonely, angry, and feel they don't have a right to feel this way because everything looks great from the outside. Just because everyone in the relationship is *doing* what they "should", doesn't mean anyone is *being* real or kind, or is vulnerably expressing their deepest selves in the relationship. I listen to many people who believe they need to hide their true selves to be accepted by their partner. They believe their partner would leave them if they really knew who they were. Self-revealing in a vulnerable way is a very scary and difficult thing for most couples.

The paradox is that without self-revealing you can never feel unconditionally loved. Without the risk of sharing how you feel and revealing what you want (hopes, desires, and dreams) you'll always feel invisible or at least conditionally loved. To feel unseen is to be lonely, even if there are always people around.

The goal of business is to increase the bottom line. A business with no profit is a hobby. Even customer satisfaction---the desire to please and accommodate the customer---is to keep the bottom line growing. There is a specific, quantifiable objective in having customers content, an objective that increases the value of the business.

Every once in a while, I see people who are married, just to be married. Some couples are "married in name only: Everyone knows they're married, but there's no real relationship. They have given up on having the deep experience that a loving, connected relationship can bring. There's no passion, aliveness, or joint creativity. Rather than home being a place to rejuvenate and go back out and face the challenges of life, it's a place to avoid and leave as often as possible.

Just checking the "married" box on a tax return or living under the same roof with someone does not mean there's an alive, caring relationship. I find that with those who've decided to settle for mediocrity, there's an underlying sense of sadness. Many lonely partners hide their pain in addictions, exciting distractions, building new projects, planning trips, and losing themselves in volunteer projects, children or grandchildren to escape the excruciating pain that settling can bring. The hunger for connections in many partners is as much a driving force as breathing and eating.

The more each partner is honest with themselves about what they value in a relationship, the more likely they'll be to be able to write or talk about it. These traits, qualities or experiences are unique and don't need to be things other people would understand.

Exercise:
Consider what is valuable about your partnership.

Examples

Boardroom:

"Everyone can see you don't treat me like you should."
"Why can't you be like my friend's partner?"
"It isn't worth my time trying to talk to you."
"I give you so much. But you don't do the
things for me you used to do."

Bedroom:

"I'm so glad you're able to listen to me without being defensive."

"I feel like I can be myself around you, and you get it."
"I love coming home and having dinner with
you. It's what I look forward to all day."
"I know your family doesn't 'get' us. I'm
glad we're who we are together."

Written Exercises:

Describe a time you felt lonely and invisible, even
when there were lots of people around.
Write a paragraph describing what "success"
in your relationship means to you.
Have your partner do the same.
Read them out loud to each other and discuss what steps you'd
like to commit to toward creating your own kind of "success."

Chapter Nine

The "Fair" in Fair Trade

We were all told as children to play fair. We complained as teenagers that our parents weren't fair. We fight for the fair treatment of our own kids. We work hard to make sure we're getting a fair deal. We're heard "all is fair in love and war." As reasonable as all that sounds on the surface, making fairness a top priority may be stealing the affection and kindness you'd like in your relationship. Most work environments post regulations about fairness. HR departments and union halls work to implement the latest fairness laws. Unfair hiring practices, monopolies and unfair insider advantages are all illegal. In most states, it's required to post nondiscrimination policies, Equal Employment Opportunity notices and injured employee's rights to medical care. Employees can retaliate and sue if certain kinds of fairness standards are not met in a business environment.

Boardrooms vote on many other kinds of fair. The fair market value of services and products, the negotiation of fair contract terms, and fair exchanges are paramount to staying in business. Treating ambitious, upwardly mobile, employees fairly is not just good ethics, but also a legally sound practice.

The idea of fairness in your intimate relationship may not seem to be any different, but it is. Every couple that's been together for any length of time has found themselves arguing about some version of fairness. We want to make sure we're not being taken advantage of, and that time, energy and money are handled in unbiased ways.

Shawn and Cyndie
"After all I do for you, you can't even do this little thing for me?" *Shawn squares his broad shoulders and grips the edge of the kitchen counter with white knuckles. The dark blue arches under his arms defy the hum of air conditioning. A scrap of paper towel is stuck to the granite with dried coffee.*

"You said I only had to go to one more of your kick back paddy-wacked tailgate frat fests," Cyndie sniped. "You haven't even tried to make an appearance at one of my gallery events!"
"My job pays for this house," Shawn snapped. "Yours is spent on your nails and the gardener. Let's be fair."
"Fair!? I put in ten times more work here than you do!" She yelled, wiping the counter with a sponge in angry circles.
"Get real. Your lifestyle would be much worse if it weren't for me," Shawn said. "Your paycheck betters my life, exactly how?"

Irreparable damage can erode a relationship when "fairness" is more important than connection. Debates about fairness are usually complaints about someone else's behavior without much self-reflection or personal responsibility for one's own feelings. *How* these discussions are handled is far more important to the overall closeness in a relationship than a *reasonable* negotiation.

There is a story in the novel "The Joy Luck Club," about a young woman's mother who comes for a first visit to the modern home of her daughter and her new husband. The daughter explains that paying equally and fairly keeps their love pure from feeling dependent or taken advantage of. The daughter only owns a small portion of the house since she doesn't make as much as her husband. He is allowed to make all the decorating decisions because he owns the bigger portion. The mother is appalled that her daughter is paying for half the ice cream bill, as the daughter doesn't even eat ice cream. The husband won't share in the flea bill because the cat is hers, even though he bought it for her as a gift.

The daughter's relationship is sterile. There's no passion, no aliveness, no romance, but it's financially equal, right down to the last cent. The story shows the mother's deep sadness for her daughter's loneliness in this just and egalitarian marriage.

Navigating this particular difference between personal and business relationships can be difficult for couples, especially if one partner has experienced losses or betrayals in the past. Many people think if they get the rules right, everything will work out in a relationship. It seems *so* reasonable that fair should lead to safe. Unfortunately, nothing could be further from the truth. Emotional safety comes from believing that your partner will give you the benefit of the doubt and have your back. Intimacy in relationships is achieved by discussing feelings, especially uncomfortable ones, like the fear of being taken advantage of. Feeling safe to share your hopes or emotional pain is more productive than weighing and re-weighing who's contributing the most.

This doesn't mean one partner can take advantage of the other by detouring every discussion back to their emotions. Acknowledging a partner's feeling is not the same things as ignoring your own, and it's not taking responsibility for theirs. But until there's a calm, mutually respectful conversation, the feelings of unfairness are likely to continue no matter what compromises you make.

When anything in business is equally divided, the two halves should look pretty much the same. The balance in a relationship, however, is more like the tides of an ocean. If a couple plans to be together long-term, change is inevitable. The very idea that anything could possibly be stationary and equal ignores that individuals change, situations change, finances change, families change, and health conditions change. The division of labor and finances that seemed comfortable to each partner before kids, or before a move, or a return to school, or before a devastating loss, or before retirement, or before an accident or illness, may not feel so comfortable now. What once felt fair could someday build resentment.

Couples that are respectful navigate these ever-changing situations in life with conversations that contribute to both partners feeling lucky to be in their relationship. Developing the ability to listen to each other while working through the fear of becoming resentful (feeling things are unfair) is the best protection a couple can have when faced with life's inevitable changes. One thing in life is certain: change. Loving couples accommodate the changes that living together for years brings.

Couples that are observant and talk about change, their own

transitory emotions and each other's dynamic dreams, paradoxically feel more stable and grounded in their stable partnerships.

Along with the notion of fair being a moving target, it's also a subjective one. When we're overworked, overwhelmed, exhausted, sick, unsure of ourselves, scared or disappointed, we tend to focus on fairness, believing it will make us feel better. When we don't know what else to do we tend to see everyone else as having it easier. This subjective inequity is often born out of our own frustration.

Remembering that we see the world though our own eyes, can help initiate conversations be less defensive. It gives us compassion that our partner also has their own expectations and preconceptions. That's not to say that we've arrived at our conclusions without justification, but the proof is our own life experience and interpretations of what we view as fair.

Many couples spend their entire marriages accusing each other of not doing as much as they do. "My owie is bigger than your owie." The arguments are about continuously changing topics, but always about making the other partner responsible for their feelings. The unspoken assumption is if they can prove they've got it tougher, the other partner has to acquiesce to what they want. They try to get nurturance through pity. Around and around they go year after year. It's exhausting and creates loneliness and bitterness.

There's a saying that good relationships are not 50/50, they're 80/80, meaning both partners will feel like they're contributing more. Comparing contributions and what each partner brings to a relationship will kill intimacy. In reality, if a relationship is in trouble, focusing on equality and fairness can be the final nails in the coffin.

Exercise:

Consider the comparisons you'd like to
let go of in your relationship.

Examples

Boardroom:
"I paid for the last dinner. It's your turn to pay."
"Look at all I do for you! What do you do for me?"
"If this relationship is going to be fair, you have to let me have some time to myself, too!"
"I spent three hours today running around doing things for your family. Why can't you put in two hours and watch this movie with me?"

Bedroom:
"When we discuss what we're going to do together on the weekends, I feel close to you."
"When you give me a little notice about going to play golf, I feel important to you."
"If I do that again, I'll build resentment. We can discuss it, but right now I don't want to do it again."
"I've let myself get caught up in comparing what we do. I don't feel so happy right now. What I want is to have you tell me how much you appreciate what I do."

Written Exercises:

Write a paragraph acknowledging where you feel things are unfair in your relationship.
Write another paragraph discussing how you can accept your partner just the way he/she is, without making him/her wrong? (What would you need to change about your perspective? What would you need to do? What would you need to say?)
Write an imaginary story about how your relationship will be in 20 years. What issues of fairness may be different? What issues of fairness are likely to be the same?

Chapter Ten

Best Friend and Companion or Balance Sheet Asset?

In literature we find plenty of examples of where business goals eclipse those of companionship. *"In business, sir,"* said he, *"one has no friends, only correspondents."* The Count of Monte Cristo by Alexandre Dumas

I don't believe people have to choose between being successful in their work or being happy at home. Strong partners understand that encouragement in the midst of a struggle can help create magnificent outcomes, both at home and in the work place.

Creativity and persistence are enhanced by someone who loves cheering you on. The less obvious solutions at the start of a struggle can suddenly show up when fear and anxiety are decreased by talking about them. These synchronistic finds happen more often when we feel safe, serene, and loved. The best answers show up when we can stay hopeful and focused while "going through" a challenge with a loving partner by our side.

Creating happiness for your partner is not nearly as important as creating emotional safety. We're responsible for creating our own happiness. Active support from a partner doesn't mean they do the work for you. It means that you aren't alone, don't feel invisible, and that you have a loving sounding board as you work toward your goal. Being connected to an unconditionally loving muse helps you believe the best about yourself and your capabilities. It provides a safe place to return home where you can lick your wounds and regroup when things don't go as expected. A caring partner shares in celebrating when you achieve your dream.

A best friend partner *is* an asset. If nurturing your emotional connection is a high priority, you won't walk alone on your life's journey, a journey which will likely see the rise and fall of fortune through the years. A best friend and lover will be there with you as you sort out your feelings and figure out what you're going to do about a difficult situation. This is a priceless asset on life's bumpy path.

In business, assets are accumulated, counted and traded for other things. Relationships, on the other hand, are about relishing a safe environment where we feel special and important and can be ourselves. A supportive atmosphere makes unlikely dreams seem more feasible.

When that supportive arena feels threatened, couples often fight. Underneath every argument lies the same question: "Am I still special and important to you?" This question may be masked by issues like money, sex, in-laws, parenting, taking out the trash, picking up clothes, etc., but really, it always boils down to feeling special and important. Believing you are special and important to your partner is a treasure that will enhance every other possession you acquire.

Being told, "You *should* feel special and important," will only create a defensive and hostile environment. Hearing, "I'd feel special and important if you did that for me," will drive a partner further away. Each partner wants to feel unique even if the gestures that make one partner feel important wouldn't do the same thing for the other. Listen carefully to what your partner says makes him/her feel special. Don't try to figure out why the list is different from the things that help you feel special. (*The Five Love Languages: How to Express Heartfelt Commitment to Your Mate*, by Gary D. Chapman, is a great place to start.)

You may never completely understand why a particular action or gift is interpreted as something that makes your partner feel loved and important to you Just remember, you're one in seven billion, and so is the special person you chose to go through life with. The way to treasure this rare connection is to share your internal state. This takes courage and vulnerability. It takes digging deep and sharing the things you keep hidden from acquaintances. It takes patience. It takes coming back and readdressing issues later. It takes commitment.

Sometimes it's easier to tell your partner what makes you feel special and important in writing rather than in person:

MyOtherHalf@love.com:
When I step out of the shower and the towel is fresh out of the dryer.
The loving silence between us when we just sit and read, touching hands.
Talking deeply about what is on each other's minds.
When we're cradled in each other's arms and I know we'll make it no matter what.
When you're busy and still notice that I'm around.
Your sense of justice.
The fresh strawberries and chocolate we had for dessert.
The insight I share with you from the book I'm reading.
When you wear the new t-shirt with the funny saying I bought.
When you make me laugh.
I'm a better version of myself when I'm with you.

Exercises:

What qualities you enjoy about your partner? What makes him/her irreplaceable?
What do you do together that reminds you of
why you chose him/her in the first place?

Examples

Boardroom:

"Don't be ridiculous. I don't have time to explain my day to you. You'd never understand."
"If you just did your part, I could do mine."
"I could get ahead if you just pitched in.

You expect me to do it all!"
"I'd be better off with that person I dated before you."

Bedroom:

"When I'm angry with you, I don't feel like having sex. Can we talk about this?"
"When I'm angry with you, I feel like having sex would help us make up. Can we talk more later?"
"I know I've told you before, but I love getting flowers. I feel really special when you send them to me!"
"I like it when you have the kids put my tools away after they use them. I feel like we're on the same team."

Written Exercises:

Write a paragraph about how you'd like your partner to be more fully present when you're struggling with something. Write a paragraph of one way you're committed to creating emotional safety for your partner when he/she is stressed, even possibly blaming you for their stress.

Chapter Eleven

Rushing to Get to the End of the Dance

"Life is what happens to us while we are making other plans."
Allen Saunders

Having been raised in a religious culture that frowned on competitive sports, I get a bit of a rebellious thrill out of my sport, dragon boat racing. I enjoy the synchronized practices out on the Pacific Ocean with 20 team members all working together. Even better are festival (race) days: The adrenalin is high and there's a sense of being connected to a sport over 2000 years-old. Excitement sizzles up the line of long boats, each decorated with a dragon head holding a metallic ball in its mouth. At the start of each festival, there's a ceremony to paint pupils in each dragon eye to mark the awakening of each boat.

At my last race, a competitive team called "Blind Start" invited sighted paddlers to fill in some empty seats in their boats. The only contingency was we had to wear blindfolds to meet the criteria for their division. With my sight blacked-out, I was led down the sandy slope to a boat. As stroker, I was to set the pace of the boat's paddling. I made my way to the front of the boat and sat on the right side of the first narrow bench.

A sighted drummer sat facing me up on the bow, seated on a tiny wooden stool. Her ancient, Chinese-style drum was inches from my black mask. She pounded the drum and counted off each time my paddle hit the water. When we neared the start line, I had to trust our sighted steersman, standing at the back of the boat, to tell me when the face of our dragon was muzzled into the net marking the start of our lane.

A horn blared and we were off. My teeth rattled with the reverberation of each drum beat. I felt the resistance of the water with each stroke. It was a dark world filled with overlapping sounds, smells of the ocean and the feeling of being propelled over the water. Time stood still. Maybe because I couldn't see the finish line, maybe because it was like no experience I've ever had, for whatever reason I was one with the boat, the ocean, the team. 2000 years of history blocked out every anticipation about the finish line.

Then I heard it: the drum of the boat on our right and the *swoosh, slurp, swoosh* of its paddles. My heart beat in my temples and I clenched my jaw, the drum beat slipping beside and then drifting just behind me. The shouts in both boats from the drummers spurred us on. The shrieks from the finish line were cattle prods and trophies all at the same time. In total darkness, I had no trouble understanding we'd placed.

The gift of this experience not only gave me the opportunity to stand in the shoes of another, which I believe is basis of all compassion and connection, but I experienced the power of being completely absorbed in the moment.

We're so focused on getting to efficient outcomes in our culture. We plunk away at drug store computers for one-minute photos. We sit in air-conditioned cars in lines for fast food. We drive up for quick oil changes. We make sure there's Wi-Fi for our instant e-mails. And the prized possession in a family room is the remote that changes the environment at the press of a button. Many couples have nothing else to talk about if they aren't discussing what needs to be done and what's the fastest way it should be completed.

To go as fast as possible through an issue in a relationship is to not have a relationship. It's like replacing a meal at a fine dining restaurant by taking a pill that makes you feel full. You'd miss the experience. The purpose of going to a lovely restaurant is for the experience.

No, we don't usually want to savor conflicts, but being able to feel loved while talking about issues *is* the essence of an emotionally healthy relationship.

We don't worry if we'll have more valuable information by the end of a good novel. We don't hurry to get to the end of a music CD we like. We don't hurry to get to the end of a walk with someone we love. Most of us have memories of getting lost in moments as kids. We were amazed at blowing bubbles and watching them pop. We could become lost in the rumble and massiveness of a train car. We knew instinctively as children how to be in the moment, but somewhere we were taught that if our actions weren't purposeful, they didn't matter. We were scolded if we "wasted time," or daydreamed. "What are you going to do?" and "When will you be finished?" relatives asked.

If you only rode on rides at an amusement park for the destination, it would be ridiculous to get on one. We ride roller coasters and sit in oval, swiveling modules for the experience, not the destination. "Where will this roller coaster take me?" isn't a question many ride operators would answer. Carnival rides are for creating an experience, not arriving at an outcome.

It's not that relationships have no goals, but people are usually in relationships for the *experience* of being connected and loved. Most of my clients are in relationships for companionship, not to go to a dinner party, visit a museum, or eat at a particular restaurant, but to have a caring companion and to feel seen and understood.

Sometimes working out differences or misunderstandings may be a longer or more difficult process than each partner expected. This doesn't necessarily mean they should spend hours and hours arguing. In fact, couples that fight until 2:00 in the morning believing they shouldn't go to bed angry, are using this old adage to justify verbal abuse. They're using it to defend wearing their partner down with redundancy and fatigue. This has no chance of creating closeness and intimacy. When we're tired, there's no real listening that happens. Throwing evidence back and forth all night is not only impolite to your partner, but also to yourself.

There are times when going to bed angry or frustrated is the kindest thing you can do for your relationship. If you or your partner is feeling angry, frustrated or disappointed, that's how you feel. Period. To pretend you or your partner can come up with good enough evidence to talk yourselves out of that feeling is futile. Feelings are alogical by their very nature.

To insist a partner discuss and work out a solution to your hurt feelings right now is disrespectful. It places the relationship in a boss/employee skew ("You must talk about what I tell you to talk about, for as long as I tell you to talk about it!" etc.). Whenever there's a power skew in a relationship, there'll be a loss of respect and partnership. Don't demand an outcome.

Being present in the moment with your partner specifically means you *do not* focus on resolution and making up quickly. A tenacious fixation on getting a partner back to being happy as fast as possible is the most common reason couples fight. They're trying to say, "If you only looked at the my facts you'd feel better right now!"

Intuitively, it seems like helping your partner feel better quickly would be the kindest thing to do. Unfortunately, it's the strategy most likely to become disrespectful, even abusive. There may be hidden fears, secret scars, and things that are hard to talk about. *How* you discuss the issue will determine how you view the interaction later, not that you came up with a fast answer. Get rest. Eat a good meal. Wait. Exercise. Spend time in nature. Be quiet and settle your own thoughts. Be kind to yourself. Allow the time needed to create closeness and safety as you work out problems. It's the dance you'll remember; don't rush to get to the end.

There's nowhere to get to on the dance floor. It's about enjoying the music and being in each other's arms. Pay attention to the special things you learn about your partner when they're in pain. Be their sounding board, their rock, their enthusiastic support. Don't personalize their struggle. If you find you're defensive or judgmental, ask yourself what their challenges are reminding you of in yourself. What we're most upset about in others are the things we still are working out in ourselves. Ask yourself how you can be more fully present in the moment and what distractions tend to pull you toward rushing, scolding others for moving too slowly or seem important enough to justify being disrespectful.

After much self-reflection, a highly motivated director came up with this about his relationship:

Being present to me means:
I love people. I can chat for hours with strangers I've just met at coffee shops or in social situations, at friend's homes and parties. It's hardly ever an issue (unless we talk about politics!). Last week, my partner Ted and I had a long talk. He told me he has a tough time at parties, and feels his best in one-on-one situations. He's not great with small talk, so he tends to hide in the corner. I was glad we could turn off the TV, put down the video game and just talk about this difference without needing to change each other or try to protect the other one from how we naturally feel.

Exercises:

Notice when you're in a rush to have your partner understand you or "see" you correctly.
Pay attention to times it feels like this could be the very last fight and you'll never get another chance to defend yourself.

<u>Examples</u>

Boardroom:

"Either you like it or you don't. Make up your mind!"
"Just admit I was right and we can end this. Don't be so stubborn."
"If you were really sorry, you wouldn't have done it in the first place!"
"Stop wasting time, just get to your point."

Bedroom:

"I feel lonely. I'd like to put some time together on the calendar."
"I get scared remembering how my parents fought. Sometimes they didn't speak for days. I don't want that for us."
"I don't need anyone to "fix" this for me. I just want to know you're here with me while I figure this out."
"It sounds like you feel strongly about this and know what you'd like to happen."

Written Exercises:

Write about a time you would've liked to take a break from an argument. What could you say about a reconvening time? How would you have kept your word to reconvene at the time you said?

Chapter Twelve

Human Beings vs. Human Doings

There were dark times in history when how one saw being vs. doing could mean the difference between life and death. One of my Mennonite ancestors was martyred over their belief on this topic. During the reformation and for years to follow, Christian theologians hotly debated whether one had to do good things or whether just *being* forgiven was sufficient to get to heaven. This has sometimes been labeled salvation through works vs. salvation by grace or faith. Another spin on this same argument- -being predestined for salvation vs. obeying commandments and behaving well—eventually exploded into a murderous frenzy. For our purposes here, an emphasis on *being* or *doing* is not a matter of life and death, but it is much more important than most communication theories or relationship therapies give it.

Annual reviews that examine whether individuals or teams have hit their numbers, or board meetings that critique if anticipated quarterly projections have been attained, are examples of *doing.* Industry competitions such as technology and medicine trying to be the first in new ventures are as well.

An often repeated quip indicating the opposite, "Don't just do something, stand there," was said to be first attributed to producer, Martin Gabel during a rehearsal of *The Assassin* in 1945. "Stop and smell the roses," is another.

It's easy to determine if something is getting *done*. It's harder to tell about a state of *being*. Most of the couples I see are interested in spending their lives with someone who cares about them and believes in them. They want to bond with a special person and *be* in love. No one can *do* enough to attain this kind of connection. It can't be purchased. No one can *do* sufficient activities to endear a partner. In fact, many of the most abusive relationships I see are perpetuated by the abusive partner holding "Look at all I *do* for you!" over the other's head. All the *doing* in the world cannot make up for *being* mean or insensitive. "What have you done for me lately?" is a question lacking love. A close loving relationship requires *being* a certain way.

Humor sometimes make the point best. In 1968 columnist Paul Crume commented in "Dallas Morning News," about some graffiti that had been incrementally created by three individuals. The first was a local businessman in Richardson, Texas

Bud Crew says that a month ago he wrote this on the warehouse wall at Bud's Tool Cribs in Richardson:
"'The way to do is to be.'—Leo-Tzu, Chinese philosopher."
A few days later, a salesman wrote under that:
"'The way to be is to do.'—Dale Carnegie,"
Recently, says Crew, an anonymous sage has added still another axiom: "'Do be, do be, do.'— Frank Sinatra." website.]

You've probably seen other versions of this on tee shirts and coffee mugs. But it's a good way to remember that *doing* and *being* are not the same thing.

Doing does not bring intimacy. We can hire people to *do* things for us: Yard work, house cleaning, child care, household repairs, fixing the car, meal preparation, laundry; most activities in life *could* be hired out.

Being is another matter. You cannot hire someone to *be* your best friend. You cannot hire someone to feel like the luckiest person in the world to *be* with you. You cannot hire someone to *be* in love with you. You cannot hire someone to *be* fully present with you in your relationship.

While *doing* may flow naturally from different states of *being,* *being* is almost never arrived at by *doing.* In fact, single people have radar for those who are trying too hard. The *doing* feels pressured and reeks of ulterior motives. People wonder, "Why don't they just *be* themselves?"

You cannot get a partner to *be* in love with you by insisting that they *do* things for you. This may seem obvious; however, it remains the number one goal of couples in therapy. You also cannot get a person to return to old feelings of *being* lucky to be in a relationship with you by focusing on what they are *doing* or *not doing*. You cannot command love. You cannot threaten someone into feeling safe with you.

It's hard to let go of focusing on *doing*. It can feel confusing and baffling, but I invite you to think about what it would mean to you in your relationship. Sitting with the frustration of a seemingly impossible quandary has been a teaching tool of Buddhist masters for centuries. Zen kōans are examples of questions that force the mind to come up with new strategies. Struggling with kōans such as, "What is the sound of one hand clapping?" "What is the color of the wind?" or "What is the half-life of time?" create new ways of problem solving. Just contemplating the question, "How can my relationship be better if I don't *do* more?" is a good place to start. An even better question is: "How do I need to *be* in order to feel close again?"

Developing strategies to avoid *doing* and *outcome* conversations when things are tense, is one of the most effective communication skills a couple can develop. All of the "what you should be *doing*" conversations in the world have little chance of creating closeness.

Being together happens when it's okay to share and both partners accept responsibility for their own feelings. Blaming, pointing out faults, and keeping score all move the focus back to *doing*. To *be* present takes practice. *Be* patient with yourself and your partner.

"Life isn't about getting and having, it's about giving and being."
Kevin Kruse

Exercises:

Slow down.
Walk slower.
Eat slower.
Write slower.

Examples

Boardroom:

"You don't *do* anything around here!"
"I do everything for you. What do you do for me?"
"There is so much to do! How can you just sit there?"
"You never give me credit for what I do!"

Bedroom:

"I'd like to just sit here with you for a while. Do you have time?"
"I'm glad you know who you are. I'm sometimes
baffled about the things you come up with, but I
love that you're not just trying to please me."
"I feel so rejuvenated just having dinner with you. Thanks."

Written Exercises:

List three ways you tend to judge your partner based
on what they're *doing*, rather than *being*.
How would you like your partner to *be* when
difficult emotions are being discussed?
How would you like to *be* when conflict arises?

Chapter Thirteen

I Don't Care What Kind of Stone You're Throwing at Me

We've all heard, "It's not what you said, it's how you said it!"

If someone hits you with a rock, you're probably not going to care much about what kind of rock it was. A geological analysis likely never crossed your mind. You just want them to not throw any more. If that person carried a rare stone with cradled hands, nestled on black felt, however, you'd be much more likely to be curious.

How we get things across to our partner is often more important in the long run than what the message is. Facial expressions, voice tone, eye contact, body language, volume, breath, gestures, may speak decuples over your message.

In business, this is less true, but still important. What you think of your boss may not be as important as them giving you all the necessary information you need to do your job. The social skills or bed side manner of professionals is less important than their competency, but with loved ones, the process is the message. We listen to those closest to us for validation and connection, even when they're talking about other things.

It's harder to focus on *how* we talk about things in a relationship than it is to focus on *what* is talked about. It's easy to get bogged down in the concrete content of conversations even when we see it's not getting us what we want.

Because numbers and observable activities can be counted and pointed at, it's easier to talk to partners about them. We can see if they took out the trash, picked up their socks or dry cleaning, contributed as much as we did to the last party, fixed a meal, or got home on time. It's harder to determine if they feel emotionally safe with you, if they feel lucky to be with you, if there's still passion and excitement. These are harder questions to face, and many of the answers may be nonverbal.

As difficult and uncomfortable as these may be, the communications that goes along with your words is what relationships are built on. It's important to convey that you care about them when you're pointing out actions you wish they'd change. If getting compliance right now is more important than closeness in the long run, you'll pay a heavy price. If telling them about what you want overrides a tone that says "You're still my special person," they may not hear a word you say.

Process-based conversations--the kind that leave you feeling safe and loved--are likely to be multifaceted, filled with ambiguity, and not spreadsheet-friendly. This is normal, at times frustrating, and completely acceptable. It's not just lovey-dovey talks that create closeness. Conversations that are self-revealing and honest, even the ones that may not be what you or your partner wants to hear, can still feel real. Connection is when partners can respect each other, even when what they're telling each other may be scary or disconcerting.

Staying fully present when you hear something uncomfortable is a developed skill. It doesn't come naturally. Riding down that first flush of adrenaline may take a while, but being able to stay compassionate and resist throwing out facts, is one of the most important closeness-building tools you can develop.

A self-reflective husband once said:

"When I complain about the things you do, please understand that I'm really just talking to myself. If it gets a little loud, it's because I'm not listening like I should."

Sometimes these styles of communication are seen as male and female differences. There are many examples of this being true. In my practice, I see dual career couples, couples that own a business together, and same sex couples. I find just as many women as men fall into the, "This needs to be fixed and I don't care right now how

I sound," scenario. Either partner can become focused on content and forget to be polite.

What we say doesn't have half the impact as the emotion we express while we're saying it. Text messages and e-mails have even made this more complicated. Don't use short cuts. Use emoticons, be clear about your emotional state, use feeling words. Express the connection you wish to maintain.

Process is the vehicle that carries the content. Make sure you give the vehicle its due. The topic may change in tomorrow's conversation, but the tone you used to convey it will be remembered.

Men and women, extroverts and introverts, may go about these process vs. content conversations differently, but ask any couple in trouble, "Was he/she being nice when they told you that?" and both men and women can recognize when the "point" is more important than respect and kindness.

Exercise:

Think of a time you felt supported and admired by someone, but you don't remember exactly what words they used.

<u>Examples</u>

Boardroom:

"You aren't wearing *that,* are you!?"
"If you really cared, I wouldn't have to ask you."
"Can't you ever use common sense? Just do
it right the first time...like I said!"

Bedroom:

"I wish you felt less anxious. I know I can't fix

this for you, but I wish that I could."
"I like it when I feel safe with you."
"It looks like you're upset. Would you like me to
hold you and you can tell me about it?"

Written Exercises:

Close your eyes and picture the last tension-filled conversation
between you and your partner. Notice where you feel tension
in your body. Notice how your breathing changed.
Write a paragraph describing different tones you use in speaking
to your partner. Which ones do you want to nurture?

Chapter Fourteen

Have Your Emotions. Don't Let Them Have You

"Flare up like a flame
and make big shadows I can move in.
Let everything happen to you: beauty and terror.
Just keep going. No feeling is final.
Don't let yourself lose me."
"Go to the Limits of Your Longing" by Rainer Maria Rilke,
translated by *Joanna Macy* + *Anita Barrows*

My parents didn't use drugs or alcohol, but I grew up in a chaotic angry household. They were raised in violence and later had written encouragement from the parenting guide written by the prophetess and founder of their religion. My uncle once described the beatings my father took as a child as so severe, they often kept him home from school. After my grandmother died when my mother was eight, her father made a habit of beating his new girlfriends so badly, that my great-grandmother would have to drive them to the hospital. Neither of my parents had models for compassionate parenting.

At nine, my brother twisted the gas cap off of the Puget [What is this?] in the garage and huffed the fumes to cope with the random beatings. When I was fourteen, my brother had finally had enough of "spare the rod, spoil the child." He and a friend "borrowed" his mother's car and drove 300 miles to Bakersfield, broke into an apartment and got drunk on "the giant evil of intemperance." Hearing all the commotion, a neighbor called the police. To release my brother the juvenile court judge had my parents agree to attend six family therapy sessions together.

I was joyous! My brother and I were isolated. We weren't allowed to play with any of the "worldly" kids on our street. We rode an hour on the bus to a religious school and back again every day. Each of the ministers my brother or I found the courage to confide in, smiled and then told our mother how insolent we were. A real therapist, even if he was from our religion, he had training in this, I was sure. Here was a chance to tell someone who would do something what was happening in our home. I poured out stories of abuse, humiliation, impulsive violence, crying myself to sleep, waking screaming in the night, and all the other hidden chaos in our conservative Christian home.

At the end of the mandatory six sessions, the young therapist had us all sit in a circle and he gave us his conclusions. He didn't suggest we attend more therapy, or that my parents take some classes or read a book. He didn't suggest parenting tools to create more predictability in the house. He didn't discuss self-care so my parents would be less stressed. He didn't even suggest any traditional communication skills. All he said was, "Well, you might want to let the kids watch a little TV once in a while and you should all pray more."

I was appalled.

I knew without a doubt I could do a better job than this guy. I subscribed to Psychology Today and hid the magazines under my mattress, because the pictures on the covers were "satanic".

This is how life purpose often begins. I decided to be a psychologist. I left home as soon as I graduated from eight grade and worked all summer at a self-supporting boarding school. The school had its own dairy, poultry farm, corn fields, commercial laundry business, bookbindery, and packaging factory. All the staff lived on campus in housing and all the students lived in dorms. My tiny, ninety-five-pound frame wrangled a floor scrubbing machine that stripped wax from the dorm room floors in 104° heat.

Before the electricity was cut at 10:00, I set a wind-up alarm clock to wake me before it was turned back on. I hiked in the dark at 5:00 in the morning to the cafeteria where I did prep work and ran the industrial dish machine. When the school year began, I worked early mornings, afternoons and evenings, around classes and homework to pay my tuition.

At sixteen, I started college. At twenty-four, I finished my Ph.D. in psychology. At twenty-five, I was licensed as a Marriage, Family, Child Therapist, and at twenty-six, I was finally licensed as a clinical psychologist.

The strong emotions of my childhood could have been my excuse to self-destruct. I could have followed in my parents' footsteps. I could have hidden my emotions in some addiction. I could have looked for someone to make it all okay and relinquish responsibility for my life. Instead of letting my emotions have me, I had them, and used them as the fuel to feed my dreams.

Emotions are complicated things. We can have some conscious awareness of them and even some conscious awareness of where they come from, but much about the character and origin of feelings is a mystery to ourselves and others. When someone is asked they feel a certain way, "I don't really know," is probably the most honest answer.

Work environments need to figure out cause and effect to keep production efficient and safe.
If a work supervisor asks, "What happened here?" the answer cannot be, "I don't know."

All of our feelings are real. They're part of being alive and the human experience. They are our own reactions to our own interpretations of things we think about, or that are going on around us. We cannot have a *wrong* emotion. We can't feel some feeling *too intensely.* When I hear a client ask, "Why do they feel that way?" I usually interpret that to mean, "Give me a justification for how they feel!"

Unfortunately, much of what elicits our emotional reactions is unconscious. We all have genetic sensitivities or resiliencies to external stimuli. We all have childhood experiences that we may or may not recall. We all have cultural biases, most of which we are not aware of. We all have fluctuations in blood sugar levels, hormone levels, fight or flight chemicals, sleep patterns, and physical stress levels. All of these significantly impact emotions, and most are completely out of our awareness when we are having a discussion.

Most of what someone says after being asked why they feel a certain way is a partial explanation, usually defensive, of what they believe will substantiate whatever it is they're feeling. This socially appropriate answer may be accurate, but may still only account for a small percentage of all the factors that played a part in creating the feeling.

One of my favorite questions to ask clients is, "Why did you put those shoes on this morning?"
I get all kinds of answers. "They are the ones I always wear," "They were at the front of the closet," "They go with my outfit," etc. Asking "why" will usually elicit socially acceptable answers, but ones that rarely have anything to do with what was really going on in someone's mind at the time they made a decision or felt a feeling. Emotions are not directly about the facts. They come from a subjective inference about perceived facts. These unique interpretations are facets of our individuality. No two people under similar situations will have exactly the same feelings.

It's not that emotions are random. Our feelings do come from somewhere. However, because they are personal, dynamic and much of where they come from is out of our awareness, they may seem less than substantial. People who do not understand this may feel obligated to try to explain *why* they feel l a certain feeling. They don't stop and consider all the unconscious associations with events from the distant past or physical impacts on their emotional state. All the elements that go into causing a person's feeling can never be fully understood or explained.

Pushing for the origin of an emotion is not very productive. Even if someone could reveal all the various factors, by the time they got through describing all the ambivalences, historical associations, physical conditions, temperature factors, and concerns about sharing all this information, the feeling would probably have already changed. When we are asked to defend or justify our feelings, we usually feel disrespected and interrogated. We instinctively defend ourselves against anyone attacking our core being. There is nothing more personal, nothing more vulnerable, and nothing harder to self-reveal than our complicated emotions. These are the things we share when we feel safe and connected.

This is another reason it's so important to accept feelings--your own and your partner's--without much "evidence." Accept that emotions may seem arbitrary, but remember that is how it *really* feels right now. This acceptance is an essential ingredient of a healthy relationship. Without it, it's impossible to have a sense of connection. Embracing the mystery of all the many things we don't completely understand about ourselves, and sharing this with a partner is difficult, but it creates real relationships. Sharing a time when you might have felt the same feeling creates empathy. Asking what your partner would like from you lets them know they're not alone while they're hurting. Sometimes a partner wants to be by themselves, sometimes they want to be held and reassured. It's okay to ask.

Sometimes it' can be very uncomfortable to be present with an upset partner. I often hear patients speak about internal emotions and the outward demonstration of these feelings as if they were the same things. "She gets way too angry," really means she acts out her anger in extreme ways. "He gets upset too easy," means one can hear him yell or see him stomp off.

All internal feelings are correct. All external expressions of them are not. The acceptance of internal feelings is not the same thing as accepting an inappropriate outward expression of those feelings. Buying a gun and shooting someone is not acceptable. Throwing dishes in the house and breaking the other person's belongings is not acceptable. Name-calling, verbally berating and humiliating, days of silence, or fighting in front of the kids are not acceptable ways to show anger. Harming others, or participating in activities where one needs to later go back and make amends, are not appropriate ways to handle feelings.

When people have coping tools for their strong emotions, they then have choices about how they outwardly express strong feelings. Even anger, which is always based in fear can be dealt with. Even anger, that's a nine on a scale of 1-10 can be acknowledged.

Jim: "I'm home! Hello, anyone here?"
Leslie: "Yeah, I'm here, just a minute
already! GEEZ, hang on a moment!"
Jim: "What's wrong? I just walked in the door..."
Leslie: "There's nothing wrong with me! Why do you
always assume there is something wrong with me?"
Jim: "Wow, is everything okay?"
Leslie: "Yeah, I thought you were going to ask me if
I got the ice cream and I forgot. I thought that's why
you were calling for me when you got home."

In this example, there was probably no way Jim could have guessed Leslie was thinking about fear when he came home. There's no way at that moment he could know all the factors that added to her sensitivity about letting someone down. There was no way he could read her mind and know she was feeling bad about not picking up the ice cream, but what he did remember was that if she seemed agitated, whatever she was feeling was real and her responsibility. He asked in a way that didn't insinuate she was wrong about her feelings, but that he was curious and wanted to know what she was concerned about.

Some emotions are harder to be supportive of than others. Anxiety--the clinical name for fear--and apprehension can fuel responses that seem out of the blue. If you get caught up chasing the "why" and "what's wrong" and whether they are overreacting, you may miss the important part of the issue, that he/she is scared and needs you to know. They don't need you to figure out where the anxiety came from, just to be supportive.

People recoil from what they fear. It can be difficult to watch a loved one living with anxiety. It may be hard for them to be enthusiastic and energetic when trying to avoid what they find frightening. Most of the things people are afraid of, their partners can't do much about. People have fears of failure, humiliation, abandonment, rejection, of not having enough, of death, of illness or poverty. These fears are, for the most part, things people need to work through for themselves.

That doesn't mean while they are struggling to develop new perspectives and coping skills that they can't use the loving support of someone who cares for them deeply, but you can't do the work for them. You can't provide enough evidence, statistics, facts, success stories, etc. to ease the fears of the one you love. You can be there to say, "I believe in you. I'm here for you and if you need to talk about it, I'll listen." And that matters.

A partner practicing what to say:

A note to my one and only,
When you told me I was being too intense, it slipped in amid a huge pile of other issues we were discussing, so I was caught off-guard when I heard it. I care that you feel that way. Sometimes I express my feelings in outward ways that are intense. I just assumed that it was a part of me that never seemed to hurt anyone, so I didn't give it much thought. When you said this, the first thing that comes to mind is that when I feel upset I say or do things that might scare you. I'd never want that to happen. Can we talk when you have the time? I want to talk about ways I can express my intense feelings better and understand where I'm dropping the ball and make amends if you feel threatened in any way.

Exercise:

Catch yourself asking "why." Find new ways
to show your interest and concern.

Examples

Boardroom:

"Why do you feel so upset?"
"You have to have a better reason than that!"
"You're reacting like your dad. He's why you're this way."
"Everyone thinks you overreact. You have
no reason to feel this way!"

Bedroom:

"I'd like you to share your feelings with me
even if you don't think I'll understand."
"Would you like to share what you're
concerned (anxious, stressed) about?"
"I get worried about things, too. It is okay to be
worried. Is there anything you'd like from me?"
"I love you, even when you're scared."

Written Exercises:

What is a response you heard from your partner in the last month
that didn't seem to make sense to you or seemed over-reactive?
What fear, apprehension or concern *might*
have been behind that response?

Chapter Fifteen

Wish upon a Star, Dream of a Ferrari and Want the Dishes Rinsed

"Dreaming, after all, is a form of planning." Gloria Steinem

Even though there was a lot of unpredictable chaos in my home growing up, Christmas was always a major event. We didn't have much money for luxuries after tithes, offerings, church building donations and missionary support, but like every kid that celebrates Christmas, in early November I would start pleading for every new toy that crossed my mind.

Often my desires were met with, "If parents indulge children by gratifying their desires, it's honoring a child's wickedness." "Parents need to counteract children's every inclination toward selfishness." And "Sacrifice must be come habitual, every member of the family from the oldest to the youngest must practice self-denial to prepare for the Time of Trouble."

However, I remember one year my father saying, "Come sit down," and, in his lefty block letter printing, he patiently kept a list of each item that I begged for. He made it clear that writing down the "must have" toy of the hour didn't mean I was getting it. The purpose of his making a production of writing my wish list was to acknowledge that my wishes were always acceptable and important to him. I don't remember what I got that Christmas, but I still remember how the gift of acknowledging my wants and wishes felt.

It can be challenging to show interest and respect for a loved one's hopes and dreams, especially if they seem far-fetched. Just like emotions, they are an essential aspect of each individual. Sharing them creates closeness.

I had a patient who worked on a large international team. Most of their boardroom discussions were by teleconference. She was extremely frustrated that so much time was taken up by team members rambling on about fantastic new products or services the company could invent. None of these members were part of R and D. None of them had been given the task to research market trends. None of them was presenting the reports that they were responsible for, and none of them was looking at the company's mission. She was frustrated and came to therapy to work on her frustration so that it wouldn't impact how she interacted with this diverse team.

In business, extensively validating everyone's wishes dreams, and hopes can be a waste of time. Efficient short cuts like making suggestions to HR or joining a brainstorming committee are practical outlets for the dreamers and visionaries.

In relationships, however, finding vulnerable ways to share wishes and hopes (not whether they are viable or not) is an invitation to get to know someone better.

When relationships start out, most people are thrilled to hear their beloved share hopes and dreams such as, "I want to grow old with you," "I want to retire in a snug cabin with you in the mountains," or "Someday, I'd like us to own property." They may have even felt closer when their loved one shared an impossible dream like, "I wish my parents hadn't moved so much," or, "I wish my dad wasn't an alcoholic," or "I wish I'd seen the red flags in my last relationship." At the start of relationships, most couples give each other the benefit of the doubt that they're not expected to make every wish and want come true for their lover. They intuitively understand that shared dreams lead to feeling special.

Later, as the relationship continues, couples tend to believe that they're supposed to give their significant other everything they wish for, defend why they shouldn't have to, or even ignore the wish altogether. Wants and desires may not sound as deep as they were before: "Honey, I'd like you to take out the trash," or "I want to take a vacation," "I wish we made love more often," or "Could you pick up your towels off the bathroom floor?" may not seem to have anything in common with the daydreaming quality of dating wishes.

Every day hopes and wants are still self-expressions of each partner. The sharing or revealing of what someone wants can still create intimacy. If a partner wants to show that their spouse is loved and special, one of the best ways to do this is to actively listen to their desires without criticism or judgment. Expressions of wants and wishes are self-expressions of who someone is and who they hope to be.

I tell couples in therapy that we all have a right to want whatever we want, and that we have a right to our desires and dreams (not the right to have them fulfilled, but the right to have the inner wish or desire). When I explain that their partner has a right to ask or wish for anything, I generally get looks of confusion, if not distain. It's usually easier to first realize that you also have a right to your wants and dreams. Most people have been taught from the time they were small that they don't have a right to their wants and dreams. "You already have one," "You should be grateful for what you have," "It will just break," "I didn't get to do that when I was your age," "What's wrong with you?" "You expect everything. You're so selfish!" Shame becomes associated with sharing unpopular wants and wishes.

Fear of humiliation can keep partners from being transparent and sharing those dreams unlikely to come true. Hiding wishes, or adamantly defending why one has a right to want something, becomes a dysfunctional style of communicating which shuts down intimacy and self-disclosure. Many people feel invisible and isolated because they've never had an emotionally safe opportunity to express what they really want in a relationship. Creating a safe place for your partner and yourself to reveal what you want is an imperative step in building a strong relationship. Many Active Listening techniques, such as paraphrasing back what was heard without interpretation or quickly throwing in your own perspective, can make demonstrating acceptance easier. Being unaware of what you want yourself, or not being sure you have the right to have your own wishes, can complicate this kind of discussion.

It's not easy to start viewing the expression of wants and desires as gifts. When a partner says, "Wouldn't it be great to go to our friend's house this weekend?' It may take a bit of reading between the lines or asking outright, "Do you *want* to go to our friend's house this weekend?"
If self-awareness and respect are strong in a relationship, the answer may be, "Yes, I'd like that," or "No, that wouldn't be my preference." If confidence is lacking, or there's fear the answer may be more along the lines of, "Well, I think we *should* since they were here last month," it may be harder to get an honest, self-revealing answer.

As you can see, most of us have not been taught how to respond to questions about what we want. We tend to be defensive, give justifications from the past, or tell stories about our right to have a certain want or desire. When you realize you have an innate right to your wants and desires, you'll be able to answer, "Yes, I want to go. What would you like to do?" or "Sounds boring, what do you want?"

Once we've taken everything into consideration, we may not even choose to pursue a wish. Don't confuse the *internal* right to a desire with the *external* getting it. This mistake is the reason partners have such a hard time accepting dreams and desires in themselves and their loved ones. More on accepting "no" as an answer in the next chapter.

The opposite of acknowledging what a partner wants, is trying to talk them out of wanting it. When facing pushback after sharing a dream, we almost always feel invalidated and disrespected. For instance, if someone tells you "You should be hungry by now. I am!" or "How could you want *that?*" you would probably feel agitated, if not outright angry at the person. "Who are you to tell me what I should want?!" most of us would at least think, even if we don't say it out loud.

Like emotions, hopes and wishes are multifaceted. Many supporting and challenging factors make up the specific wants we ultimately choose to take action on in the outside world.

For example, if I'm late for an appointment and I see the light ahead of me turn red, I do not *want* to stop at that light. If someone asked me, "Is it your desire to stop at this light?" My answer would emphatically be, "No!" Do I stop? Of course I do. All things taken into account--safety, the laws, other people, keeping my driver's license, etc.--I choose to stop at the light. What we wish for, and what we eventually do, may have little in common.

Another aspect of wants to remember is that when people have strong dreams they may appear "driven" toward their goals. Partners looking from the outside may be baffled by the energy and passion displayed. They might even be tempted to see their partner as unbalanced and too intense. This may actually be true. Their actions and conclusions may make no sense to you. Their priorities may seem wrong or out of focus. You may fear they will inhibit your own dreams and desires, or leave you lonely and feeling disconnected.

These are important things to talk about (without making either of your dreams and desires wrong). When partners are supportive of each other's dreams, they can both feel fulfilled and connected, over time. When a partner is pursuing a longed-for dream, they may feel fatigued and exhausted, but there should also be some passion and enthusiasm. If you can cheer them on, being respectful of your own feelings, you are likely to be the lucky recipient of all that passion and excitement.

It can be challenging to be in a relationship where one or both partners are pursuing dreams. These may be shared dreams, such as raising a family or starting a business, or individual dreams like getting a degree or helping a cause. This is where sharing feelings (while being responsible for your own, of course) and sharing your wants and needs (accepting "no" as an answer, if need be) becomes very important to staying close.

Knowing your own passion and dream, as stated before, is an important gift to bring to your relationship. Joseph Campbell's directive, "Follow your bliss," is one of the best gifts you can give your significant other. Even if they can't follow it right now, talking about their dream, feeling supported and acknowledged, will bring you closer together.

We are not taught to view the disclosure of wants and desires as gifts or self-revealing. Most couples hear the expression of a hope or desire as a directive, skipping over the intimacy building part of self-disclosure and assuming a compromise is being demanded of them. Disclosing a dream is not the same as a demand that the dream be fulfilled.

When we know we have the right to our inner desires and dreams, we don't need to defend them as reasonable. Our wants and dreams are expressions of the complicated beings we all are. Our wants and our feelings are inner states, and very personal. Listen to your partner. Share your hopes with them, holding them with an open hand, detached from an outcome. It's the self-revealing that creates closeness, not necessarily getting what you want.

Ruminations brought to you by the Great Recession:

When I tell Jerry that I want something, his first reaction is always to tell me that I don't.
I don't know the exact reasons why he does this--and I suspect that he doesn't either, if he's even aware of it--but I think that it's because we're having a tough time financially, and since I lost my job, he always equates wants and needs with "How much is this going to cost me?"
There's a certain amount of Jerry's identity wrapped up in making things happen, getting the food on the table and being a provider, you know?
So while I can guess where this comes from, or at least why

he says it, I have a tough time confronting him, because I know he's trying to do right by us, and that just adding to his pressure isn't going to make things any better. In the end, though, what he doesn't understand is that it ends up with me feeling bad for saying what I want and him trying to control me, even if he's not aware that he's doing it.

Exercise:

What response (behavior) have you heard (seen) in the last month from your partner that seemed "driven" and headed for some goal "at any cost?"

<u>Examples</u>

Boardroom:

"You want everything! Can't you ever just say 'Thank you'?"
"How could you want *that?* Didn't you read
the article about it last week?"
"No one ever succeeds at *that*. Don't set
yourself up for disappointment!"
"You only want one of those because you friend
(mother, father, cousin, neighbor, etc.) wants one!"
"You wish I was someone else!"

Bedroom:

"It sounds like you wish I'd change my mind."
"I wish we could talk about this in a respectful way."
"I want so much to say this in a way you'll
understand that I don't think you're wrong"
"I'd like us not to both be so angry all the time."
"I wish I had the self-confidence to not get
so defensive when I get scared."

Written Exercises:

Write a paragraph describing the first time in your life you can
remember being told you had to justify something you wanted.
Write about a time in your life you were told that what you
wanted that was wrong or bad.
Write about a desire or dream you're afraid no one else will
understand or people close to you might try to talk you out of.
Write a description of the fulfillment of a special
dream you have (as though you already had it) on
a small piece of paper. Carry it with you.

Chapter Sixteen

"No" must be a respected answer

"In this world, there are only two tragedies. One is not getting what one wants, and the other is getting it." Oscar Wilde

During the recession that started in 2008, I had a client discussing a terrible downturn in sales. They were still motivated and energetic: Their motto was "A 'no' is just one call closer to a 'yes'." This attitude kept them pushing to change potential customer's minds. They believed the harder it was to get an account, the harder it was to lose it.

This is a great sales tool, a creative way to stay motivated and not define oneself by a slow market. Every company would love to have all its sales force live by this view, but in your personal relationship pushing to change your partner's "no" into a "yes" can lead to fights and resentment.

A friend of mine, a therapist who walks her talk, Dr. Dani M. Smith, is in charge of Proactive Education Encouraging Responsibility (P.E.E.R.) at Chapman University in Orange, California. Her campus projects focus on reducing sexual assault on college campuses. It probably comes as no surprise that in her freshman orientation talks she emphasizes "Accepting 'no' for an answer." She reminds the new students that California has recently passed the Affirmative Consent law. This is the most conservative law of its kind, stating that in a sexually charged situation, only a direct, clear answer of "yes" doesn't mean "no" for sexual consent. Her students learn about listening for all the ways a potential sexual partner may indicate a "no."

We can all agree that not accepting "no" for an answer in a sexual situation is rape. Couples are often surprised when I tell them that not accepting "no" for an answer in conversations is emotional rape.

Badgering your partner into changing their mind or redundantly giving evidence about why they should do something or see something your way is disrespectful. Even if you believe that it would be in your partner's best interest to change their mind, the poking and prodding may create an even worse condition than the one you were trying to fix in the first place.

There are many disrespectful ways of not accepting no for an answer:

Keeping score: "You can't stay home! I went with *you* last time!"
Worrying about what other will think: "You have to wash the car! What will the neighbors think?"
Blackmail: "If you don't do this for me, don't expect me to do you any favors!"
Humiliation: "You don't want to try this because you're a coward (bad parent, insecure, etc.)!"
Broken record: "Come on, you'll enjoy it. Really, I know you will. Just give it a try. Everyone likes it. Don't be so stubborn, you know I'm right. Please, just this once..."
Silent treatment: "Fine." *Then doesn't speak for two days.*
Threatening abandonment: "You're driving me into the arms of someone else! I don't know how long I can put up with you not doing what I ask."

Some of the clients I work with can't remember a time their partner said "no" directly. I tell them there are many ways we say "no" in life. When I say "No" to the enthusiastic girls selling Girl Scouts cookies---and I have boxes piled in my kitchen---I say, "Thanks, not today, but you're an amazing entrepreneur! Keep up the great work!" They can tell from my words and body language I'm not going to buy any cookies that day.

There are many ways someone may say, no". Any time we don't get what we want from a partner---they "forgot," they made an excuse, they changed the topic, or gave no response at all, these are still ways of saying "no."

Kelly: But you promised.

Tom: I know I did.

Kelly: I made plans.

Tom: Sorry, I completely forgot about it. I must've gotten distracted.

Kelly: So you weren't thinking of me, just yourself.

Tom: Geez, you sound upset. I care about how you feel and how you'll react, but I still can't go.

Kelly: Who'll call the Bennetts and tell them you changed your mind?

Tom: Okay, I'll call them, but I want to talk about this some more. Are you that disappointed?

Kelly: I'm not happy at all about it.

Tom: I guess I changed my mind. I don't want to go.

Kelly: But I made plans...

Tom: I know. And even if we've made plans, I still may say no, sometimes.

Kelly: I would never do that to you. Even if I hate where we're going, I'll do it for you.

Tom: Wow, I hope not. Please don't! You have the right to say no, too.

Exercise:

Watch how you feel when you think you've been clear about saying, "no" and someone ignores your choice (even if they believe that what they want you to do is in your best interest.)

<u>Examples</u>

Boardroom:

"I know if you just think about it, you'll change your mind."
"Look at the facts. You'd really benefit from this."
"You're being ridiculous. Everyone wants one."
"You're selling yourself short. You're going to regret it."

Bedroom:

"You haven't given me an answer. Are you telling me no?"
"I'm really sad you're not willing to help. I feel
confused. It seems so simple to me."
"Please let me know if it feels like I'm nagging you."
"It's okay for us to be different. You don't
have to like everything that I do."

Written Exercises:

Write about a time you felt less loved because your
partner told you "no" about something. What might
be another reason they turned you down?
Write three things you can say next time you're
tempted to force your partner to change their mind
and do/say/think what you want them to.

Chapter Seventeen

Trying to Exchange the Gifts of
Someone's Wants & Feelings

"Love comes when manipulation stops; when you think more about the other person than about his or her reactions to you. When you dare to reveal yourself fully. When you dare to be vulnerable."
Joyce Brothers

Now that I've discussed that partners have a right to say "no" I want to address the drives that sometimes make us push so hard to change someone we love.

Once again, we admire career people with the grit it takes to say "yes" to job opportunities that most other people wouldn't consider. Special forces in the military, Astronauts, and the brave physicians that go into the field to treat epidemic outbreaks, like Ebola, step up to some of life's biggest challenges.

In survival or emergency situations, it can seem like there are no alternatives, and the other person would be crazy not to accept your suggestion. No matter how dangerous or perceived dangerous a situation is, respect and patience will always lead to a better relationship. My grandparents found ways to work together even though many of the things they wanted were different and they had to cope with strong feelings that often had no immediate relief.

My paternal grandmother, Lois Nightingale, who I was named after, married the love of her life, Dan, in 1930. Even though they were in sunny Southern California, the dark background to their early life together was the Great Depression. The year before they got married, The New York Stock Exchange lost 40% of its value. The year they got married, more than 26,000 businesses failed, with many more that would follow, and the first round of banks closed their doors.

My grandmother was a private vocational nurse with a 10th grade education and my grandfather had worked in the oil fields for Standard Oil Company since he was fourteen. She left her job in Heber to move to Stanton with him, where she became pregnant. That year, in Michigan, 3000 unemployed workers marched on Ford Motor Company. The security guards and local police killed 4 and injured 60.

When my grandmother was seven months pregnant, there were food riots on grocery stores, as panicked families resorted to the unthinkable to feed their children. In May 1931, when my dad was born, the Federal Reserve's Federal Fund's rate bottomed out at 1.52%. [Source?] Between May and June, more banks were failing and people were increasingly depressed and hopeless.

By 1932, when my uncle was born, one in every four workers was unemployed and more than 10,000 of the nation's 25,000 banks had closed.] There were hunger marches and small riots as stock prices reached the lowest point of the Depression.

In 1933, private investments in manufacturing had dropped by more than 80%. The US gross national product was cut by more than 50% from 1929. [Sources?] America grasped at desperate measures. The government authorized the slaughter of six million pigs to stabilize agriculture prices. FDR ended the gold standard backing US dollars. No one knew what was going to happen.

With 13 million Americans unemployed, and two little ones in diapers, my Grandma Lois began to panic. Her doctor pressured her to eat more because she was wasting away to skin and bones from breast feeding. She was afraid if she quit nursing she would get pregnant again. She had no real information about birth control, so she asked a stranger while waiting in a grocery store line. The woman told her about vasectomies and she went home with a request.

Meanwhile, Dan had a solution to propose for their financial issues. Standard Oil Company, based in Baton Rouge, wanted to send them to Lafayette, Louisiana. She spent the next few weeks canning vegetables and fruit (they lived down the street from the Knotts farms). They packed up the car with two toddlers and drove 1800 miles. Lois had been driving her father's ice delivery truck since she was thirteen, so they took turns behind the wheel.

What she hadn't prepared for was the dire situation in Lafayette in 1935. The Depression had only added to the devastation from recent floods. Twenty-nine percent of the work force was laid off. [Source?] Although she hated the weather (I have a picture of my father and uncle floating down streets in wash pans after a storm) she loved the warm, friendly people. Having been raised on the boarder of Mexico, she was comfortable with other cultures and soon her two boys had a group of diverse friends: Cajun, black, white, Catholic, Christian and of religions from distant places.

Even though my grandfather relaxed with his HAM radio when at home, drilling wells during the hurricane seasons was hard on him. When he mentioned a transfer to Texas, my grandmother couldn't help but think about the Conroe disaster.

In 1933, an oil well blew out and erupted into flames. The runaway well cratered and completely swallowed all of the nearby drilling rigs. The crater eventually resembled a large natural lake, but at the time it had to look like a page out of hell. Dan reassured her that Oilton was nowhere near Conroe, so once again they set off, with rivaling boys, on a 550-mile drive into the panhandle of Texas. I'm not sure if my grandfather told her that they would be living 32 miles out of town, and water wasn't as plentiful as their last soggy home.

All their water (sulfured) would have to be trucked in once a month and stored in a tank. There weren't any neighbors around for miles, but there was plenty of room for barefoot eight and nine-year-old boys to roam before and after home schooling. They shot rabbits to feed their pet hawks, and brought home rattle snake eggs that they convinced their mother were turtle eggs.

Together, they fought the elements and the economy to carve out a life together. There were personal demons, as well. They each struggled to leave behind some, and retain other, aspects of their own upbringings. More about that later.

During the last financial crisis, I had the opportunity to help couples and families find ways to communicate even though everyone was scared and no one knew exactly where all the changes would stop. We all know what fear is. Most of us can describe the physical sensations of the fight or flight response, but one frustrating aspect of this reaction is the difficulty to find words. This is due to neurological changes when adrenalin and cortisol flood the body. When we are scared, there is also a tendency to view choices as black or white. This can be alienating at best, during a difficult conversation.

What these all or nothing/black and white statements insinuate is that it's "wrong" to have ambivalence. It's amazing how many adults seem to think it's a defect in character to feel more than one thing at a time, even opposing feelings, such as relief *and* sadness, etc.) Being able to speak clearly about ambivalence is necessary to have honest and self-revealing communication.

Seeing situations simplistically, or in black and white terms, perfectionism, and demands of all or nothing may be signs of addiction. Given that much of the media we see, hear, and read reflects this attitude, it's no wonder our conversations with our loved ones are modeled after addicted conversations.

In some ways it's a kind of thought disorder to believe we know how someone else should feel and what someone else should want. This is actually a form of codependency. Codependency creates terrible pain for those who have it, and it isn't too comfortable for the people around them, either. In most cases, a belief that they know how others should feel or what others "should" want comes from a strong desire to help their loved one, but pointing out other's unsubstantiated feelings and wants creates mistrust, anger, even desires for retaliation, in the person they were hoping to help. The codependent will soon feel resentful, unappreciated and exhausted as well.

It's just as detrimental to believe that your own feelings and wants are not justified. We can't have more acceptance of other's feelings and desires than we have for our own. If we don't believe we can feel terrible over some event, then we can't understand how someone else would be able to have an unsubstantiated right to them, either. Continuously doubting your own right to wish and hope will soon find you criticizing other's dreams.

Being accepting of your own feelings---however strong, intense, irrational, or unauthorized--is the best thing you can do toward accepting your partner's. Embracing and reaching for your own hopes, dreams, desires and wants, is the greatest action you can take toward remembering your partner has a right to his/her hopes and goals.

It would be a different world if it was common knowledge that we all had the internal right to feel how we feel and want what we want. We'd be dealing with reality; the reality of individuals and the dynamic nature of internal states of being. I sometimes imagine what it would be like if teens were taught that if someone told them that they had "no right to feel that way," it would be acceptable to look at the accuser with dismay, and say, "How could I not have the right to feel how I feel? Do you mean under these circumstances, you wouldn't feel the way I do right now? Or do you really mean you're afraid of how I might act in *expressing* my feeling?"

If you're in a relationship where accepting feelings and wants is still very new, make sure you have a healthy support system around you. Sometimes I see couples who are just learning that they have a right to feel how they feel and want what they want. I tell these couples it's as if they were both in ICU together, beds beside each other, and getting upset at the other one for not changing their IV.

The courage to share your large and small wishes is a gift to each other. Your trust to share your feelings, your strong ones and the ones you barely notice, with each other, will build an unbreakable bond between you.

Here's an example of a mundane conversation that builds closeness:

Jean: "Dick and Stella are going to Bermuda again next month. That's the second time they've gone in five years."
Bill: "They must be doing well."
Jean: "They planned ahead, before Dick retired."
Bill: "Sounds like you're disappointed that we're not joining them."
Jean: "I just want to get out of the house more often. That's all."
Bill: "You feel stuck?"
Jean: "A little. We're just sitting and binging on Netflix."
Bill: "I can see that."
Jean: "I want to spend more time with you and it seems like---."
Bill: "We're closer to the television than we are each other?"
Jean: "Sometimes."

Exercise:

Pay attention to the times you defend your right to how you feel or what you wish for. How could you say this more directly, without explaining yourself?

<u>**Examples**</u>

Boardroom:

"I just want an answer!"
"You can't expect me to want to have sex with you when you're always coming home late and never help with the kids!"
"You have no right to want to spend all that money on redecorating when we just took an expensive vacation!"
"How dare you ask to go to your family's for Thanksgiving, when mine have done so much for us?"

102

Bedroom:

"No, I'm not up to doing that right now, but I love
you, and what you want is important to me."
"Could you write to me and I could read
about how you're feeling?"
"Do you want to talk about what you want right now?"
"When you share your dreams with me, I
feel close to you. Thank you."

Written Exercises:

Write a paragraph about how feelings and wants were discussed
in your previous relationship. How are things different (or
similar) in your current relationship?
What qualities do you think your partner may see in you
from the perspective of his/her past experiences?
What qualities do you think you see in your partner
through the eyes of your own history?

Chapter Eighteen

Taking Poison to Hurt Someone Else

"No one can make you feel inferior without your consent." Eleanor Roosevelt

There are things we can do something about and things we can't. When we take action about the things we can and don't drain our energy focused on things out of our control we don't build resentment.

My paternal great grandfather, Jacob Nachtigall, who came to the US in 1875 only spoke Low German at home. After getting married and having six children, he became more and more upset about how his friends and family were being treated back in Russia. The Russian government had reneged on taxation exemptions and stopped allowing forestry service in lieu of military service for the Mennonites. Their large prosperous farms were divided among the peasants. Grain prices plummeted and their exclusive licenses for brewing beer were withdrawn. Many in the previously prosperous colony now poor and starving.

They were considered politically suspect and in 1918 all the men 16 to 65 were exiled in unheated freight cars to work in primitive labor camps and mines in Siberia and Kazakhstan. Religious leaders were treated worse than criminals. Anyone who died was simply thrown from the train.

It was the last straw. He completed his Naturalization papers, proclaimed German would not be spoken at home any longer and changed the family name to Nightingale. He also participated in fundraising to help the refugees.

He took action on the things he did have control over. He focused on what could be done. This helped lower his resentment and feelings of victimization.

Sometimes it's difficult to determine what is in our control and what isn't. One of the things we do have control over is how much we contribute to those we love. We are always responsible when we say, "Yes."

Resentment comes from contributing more than you're comfortable giving to someone who can't or won't keep their agreements with you.

In business agreements made with lending institutions, franchises, contractors, suppliers etc. are generally predictable and honored, if not the word gets around and they go out of business. In family relationships agreements can be far more complicated. Many so called agreements that individuals make, are all in their heads. I often hear a patient complain, "But I never do that!"

And I reply that while that may be true, it is irrelevant unless an overt agreement was made that they would do the same thing you do. I also hear clients complain that children or teenagers don't keep their word. This is part of being an immature human. Parents are responsible for raising and guiding kids. Parents should anticipate that children and teens need supervision and expect that they will sometimes (or lots of times) promise things they can't do.

Another classifications of people who may not be able to keep their agreements with you are the mentally ill, addicts/alcoholics and those who are scared of you.

If someone has blatantly lied to you, first ask yourself if there's any chance they may be afraid, or worried about your response if they'd said "No" or told you they changed their mind. While we are never responsible for others feelings, recognizing them can keep us from being surprised. Anxiety can keep many people from freely sharing their truth.

The term "Co-dependent" comes from the concept that many chemically dependent people have one or more loved ones that become anxious and agitated if they're not trying to make the chemically dependent person get better or "understand." It's not a good term for people who are caring and helpful but who do not take care of themselves first. These nurturing people suffer because they are emotionally empty and have begun to feel like victims and martyrs. Many of these co-dependents have never had a chemically dependent person in their lives.

The best clue to co-dependency is resentment. The more resentment a person has the longer they have been acting co-dependently.

Unlearning co-dependent habits and learning to take personal responsibility for one's own resentment can be a lifelong challenge. Once someone has a good case of resentment, they've probably been nursing it for a while. When we feel we've been taken advantage of, it's hard to look at the situation any other way.

When a business is wronged, a trademark infringed, a contract breached, or unfair practices used as defined by the law, if a cordial letter or call yields no results, it may take legal action. When an employee is wronged in the workplace, and HR can't solve the issue, legal action may also be available. Legal action can sometimes correct unfair activities in business. Resolution to broken promises in the work place is usually a formal process. Everyone does better if there is a course of action.

When resentment builds in relationships, most couples don't know what to do except retaliate, harangue or give the cold shoulder. All these attempts to cope with disappointment and the subsequent resentment, devastate intimacy and closeness.

When resentment builds partners tend to want to retaliate. They believe if someone else feels bad, they'll feel better. This is rarely true, and if it is, the relief is fleeting, because we're always responsible for our own feelings. Our interpretation of other's actions causes our feelings. Our own expectations make us feel angry or disappointed.

Everyone is responsible for their own emotions. Even when we can't think of ways to handle them, no one else can do it for us. Even when you're upset, there's a sense of serenity and maturity that comes with remembering your feelings are your own. Giving away responsibility for your feelings is dangerous and disrespectful to yourself. And worst of all, it will lead you to believe you're then responsible for someone else's emotional state.

Retaliation is a punishment, one that might even be intended for "teaching" purposes. Anytime one partner tries to punish or teach the other, there's an employer/employee or power skew that builds distance and resentment. It's doubtful your partner will care much about your pain if you're scolding them. They'll just be defending themselves.

In contrast, when a partner, who is taking care of themselves emotionally, demonstrates curiosity and compassion, this leads to believing their partner will also be kind and patient if *they* make a mistake.

In personal relationships we all have "a line." I call this "The line of codependency." It's an invisible line, and it moves based on if we're tired, hungry, agitated or lonely. When we take care of ourselves and feel rejuvenated, happy, empowered and connected, there's more room on the "unconditional" side of the line.

The Line of Codependency

Conditional (expect something/change, may build resentment if no agreement)	Unconditional (no strings attached, can't build resentment, part of self-definition)

We all contribute on each side of the line in some areas of life. On the side of the line that's "unconditional," we expect absolutely nothing in return. We do things because doing them is in line with our integrity and our self-definition. A parent may get up with a crying child, a driver may hand the homeless man by the road five dollars, a Good Samaritan may take a wounded animal to the vet. These people would be out of their integrity and how they define themselves if they behaved in any other way. Contributing with no strings attached means we may not even care that the receiver is aware the act of kindness came for us. Anonymous gifts, secret pals, visiting a sick friend, fixing something without expecting any acknowledgement, are all examples of contributing on the "unconditional" side of the line.

Over that line on the "conditional" side, we expect something to happen. So when we sign a contract with an account, get hired by a company, agree to do contract work, these are *not* unconditional. We expect to get paid. We make an agreement and expect something in return. This is good business practice.

The trouble comes when we decide to contribute over the line into "conditional" territory, but we *haven't* made an agreement. We go in "hoping" that the other person, will notice, care, change, reciprocate, understand, appreciate, pay attention, straighten up, stop, start or follow our lead. The list is endless of how our contributions can be tied to some expected outcome. When we contribute over this line without an agreement, our resentment builds.

This may sound complicated. We're not always aware when we have strings attached to something that we contribute, whether it's being a sounding board for our partner's venting, doing too much or contributing more money than we're comfortable giving.

The solution is making a promise to yourself and sticking to it. Keeping your word to yourself may mean saying to yourself, "If they don't pick up after themselves I can: count on myself to say how I feel, ask them if they're okay, go for a long walk, or remind myself of their good qualities." All of these are things you have control over. We have no control over other people, not even those we love.

There are times in all our lives when keeping our word is harder than others (depending on illness, work schedule, financial constraints, energy level, overload, etc.). When asking someone for an agreement, make sure you're clear that it's okay for them to say "no." Otherwise, because of anxiety and fear, you'll have no predictability. (More about this later, as well.)

For instance, Mary says to Pete, "I'm going to invite the neighbors over for dinner. I'll make the salad and dessert, if you'll barbeque."
Pete says, "We just had the neighbors over. I really don't feel like having a lot of people around this weekend. I'd like to just have some quiet time at home."
Mary replies, "But they're new neighbors who just moved in, and I want them to get to know everyone. I'm really excited about the kids having new friends to play with."
Pete: "This is the only day I'm going to have off in two weeks. I really don't want to spend it entertaining."
Mary: "Well, then I guess I'll just have to tell everyone the barbeque is off. The kids will be so disappointed."
Pete: "Okay, okay, I'll barbeque. What time is everyone supposed to invade us?"

There is a good chance that even if Pete cooks, he'll check out, emotionally. He'll be resentful that he said "yes," when he really wanted to say "no.". Mary may feel resentful because in her mind she made the arrangements, found new friends for the kids, and would be preparing part of the meal, so her unstated agreement was that Pete would be happy and barbeque. Pete is unlikely to meet her expectations.

When we push and ignore our partner's feelings and wants, we set ourselves up for disappointment. If we have to hard sell an agreement, it may not be one we can rely on, because it wasn't given from the place of a partner and best-friend. The other person may have felt there was no other way out. This is where passive/ aggressive reactions may show their ugly faces. When people stop believing they have any say in things, they may "forget" to keep their word, show up on time, or stay focused. True passive/

aggressive actions are unconscious. People really don't know they aren't doing things to feel a sense of control in their lives.

If you are contributing over your line into "conditional," and you cannot make an agreement with someone who is likely to keep their commitment, it's important to make an agreement with yourself. Then you must keep that agreement.

Let's look at Bethany and Justin.

If Bethany knows it is unlikely that Justin, her alcoholic husband, can keep his word about only having two drinks at a wedding she really wants to attend, she must make an agreement with herself.

She knows that if she attends the wedding with him and just hopes it will be better this time, it over her "conditional" line. She doesn't feel she can go with no expectations. She knows she will feel resentful if she's there when he's drunk and acting out. So she makes the agreement with herself (and tells Justin) that she will take a separate car and will leave the party early if she needs to. She explains that she doesn't want to become resentful, and that caring for herself will keep her from being resentful of him and better their relationship.

If she conveys her decision with anger or by "making him wrong," she is once again contributing over her line of unconditional, by hoping to "educate" and "change" him by her words. If he doesn't change, or see it her way, she'll be resentful that she wasted so much energy trying to convince him.

If she can accept that he may have feelings about her decision (sadness, disappointment, embarrassment) and she accepts these and doesn't try to explain away his uncomfortable feelings, there's a greater likelihood of them both feeling respected, even if they're taking separate cars.

It's possible at another time that attending a different wedding with Jason would've been on the "unconditional" side of the line. For instance, if the wedding was "dry," or they had another function to attend later and could only stay a short time. Each situation must be examined as to whether your contribution is likely to lead to resentment.

Resentment, built over time can destroy a relationship, or make it hell to live in. Resentment is an insidious poison that will drain the life and vitality out of not only the relationship, but the person holding onto the resentment. We can do very little to change other people's resentment, except be a safe place where they can vent and speak about their anger, sadness and disappointment. Remember, feeling seen and heard are no small part of assisting someone in putting down their resentment, but it's still their psychological work, and they can only do it when they're ready. No one else can speed up the process.

The Short Cut

You should know how I feel.
Even if
I have neglected to tell you.
Because that's what people
Truly in love
Do.
On television
In books
And in poetry.
They
Read minds.
But then
You'd know that
If you
Truly
Loved me.

Exercises:

Pay attention to when you say "yes," when what
you really want to say is "no," "later," "I'll get
back to you," or "maybe next time."

Board Room:

"I give and give and give, and *this* is how you thank me?!"
"With all I have done for you, the least you could do is…"
"You always have to have your way!"
 "I thought if I kept telling you, you would finally
get it. Now look at the mess you are in!"
"I have done so much for you, and you
can't do this one thing for me?"

Bedroom:

"When I feel stressed, I like it when we
do household chores together."
"It sounds like you're very angry. Are you
concerned about how I might react?"
 "I'm afraid if I don't stand my ground on this topic I'll
feel resentful. I wish I could think of another solution."
"I am going to spend more time with friends so I don't feel so
isolated."

Optional Exercises:

Write about one place you contribute unconditionally
in your life, with no expectation of return.
Write about one area in life you have let
yourself become resentful about.
Who would you need to make an agreement with to
not build any further resentment in this area?
If the agreement is with yourself, not expecting that anyone
else will change, what agreement do you need to make with
yourself? Is it one you can trust yourself to keep? (Hint: Smaller

agreements are more likely to be followed through on.)

Chapter Nineteen

I Beg Your Pardon, I Never Promised You a Rose Garden

*"Forgiveness is the perfume which flowers
give when trampled upon."*
1855, The Sacred Circle, Edited by Judge Edmunds, Dr. Dexter, and O. G. Warren,
Volume 1, Quote Page 410, Partridge & Brittan, New York. (HathiTrust)

*"If we can learn to deal with our discomfort, and just relax
into it, we'll have a better life." -Mellody Hobson*

Last year I flew to England to attend my daughter's college graduation at University of London, Goldsmith's College. Several of the buildings where she attended classes were older than the US. The ceremony was filled with elegant formalized rituals. The orchestra, colorful professorial gowns and vintage hats, even the huge ceremonial maces spoke of tradition deeper and more profound than any of my graduations. I wondered at the healing process that took place between 1776 when Daniel Chapin, my fourth great grandfather, served in the 18th Regiment of the Militia and today, where being called a "Yank" in jest, was the closest my daughter would ever come to understanding the venomous relationship between the Old World and the new one.

I don't think it takes hundreds of years to attain a forgiving heart. But I see relationships where one or both partners feel like the process is taking a hundred years.

In business it is a quicker process. There's a spot on corporate tax forms for bad debt that was written off during a fiscal year. Even though there's a tax credit for not getting paid, writing off too much debt can put one out of business. It's important to collect from customers as soon as possible and not take on a lot of bad debt. Chasing debt and getting people to pay is even an industry in itself.

Corporations can file for bankruptcy if they can't pay their debts. Well-known names in business have filed to have corporate debts forgiven and reconstructed: Henry Ford, Walt Disney, Milton S. Hershey, H.J. Heinz, Kim Basinger, Larry King, Stan Lee, and four-time winner Donald Trump. Paying off, restructuring or forgiving debt is all part of doing business.

Emotional debt, as accumulated in disappointments and broken promises, is a relationship concern. As devastating as being betrayed and let down can be, holding indebtedness over your partner's head will only further the distance back to being your best friend and partner again.

Forgiving debts in a business, or a bankruptcy court, is done over time with much deliberation, attorneys, accountants and paperwork. The debt must meet pre-established criteria and many laws dictate what may happen.

In relationships, the faster debts are dealt with, and their origins understood and forgiven, the faster a couple can move back into creating closeness and trust.

Many couples believe if they are meant to be together, that betrayal will not happen in their relationship. Unfortunately, there are only humans on this planet, all with flaws and vulnerabilities. If couples are in a relationship for more than a few months, disappointments, not meeting expectations and perceived betrayals will certainly be part of what they have to overcome.

Some deceits and disloyalties may seem small, others large, but at the core of romantic relationships is the need to feel special and important to a partner. To be in a passionate caring relationship takes being vulnerable. Laying oneself open to the possibility of being hurt takes great courage. But it is the only door to an intimate relationship.

The first time he doesn't call when he says he's going to, the first time she stays out with her girlfriends longer than she'd planned, when he confesses his "number" of previous partners is more than he said at first, when she shares that her credit cards are up to the limit, any challenge to the image of our perfect partner can make us feel betrayed.

As the relationship continues, betrayals and not meeting expectations happens more. Individuals in relationships spend too much money, call past lovers, drink too much, crash the car, hide purchases, get fearful about inheritances, go places without letting the other one know, forget to pick up milk on the way home--- the list is infinite. Couples who trust they have communication tools to get past the daily (and sometimes the once-in-a-lifetime) betrayals, develop a sense of safety and commitment that other couples can't understand.

The first step in writing off the debt is realizing that each person is responsible for their own feelings. (I know this is sounding redundant, but it's still true, even when the other person has done something terribly wrong.) As hard as this may be, the offending party cannot be fully present and listen to their partner's hurt and pain while they're busy trying their best to get the other person to see them in a better light.

On the part of the one who made the mistake, it's extremely difficult to listen with unconditional acceptance when the person you love is telling you they're in pain and it's your entire fault. There's a knee-jerk reaction to find facts and evidence to "prove" that they're not responsible for the pain of their partner. If they only could look at it from a different perspective (with different facts) they'd forgive and be comfortable and happy again.

Remember that emotional safety requires letting the other person feel however they feel (even if it's angry with you) and want whatever they want (even if it's impossible, like turning the clock back). I often hear partners who are the offending party say, "If I acknowledge their feelings I'm just giving them more fuel. They'll never get over it!"

116

Listening and acknowledging feelings does not make them stay that way they are forever. No feeling can remain stationary.

The very nature of human experience is that feelings and desires *must* change. That's why commitment is a better indicator of how a relationship is doing than how partners feel at the moment. Allowing and being compassionate of uncomfortable, even excruciating, feelings in a relationship creates a sense of unconditional acceptance and love. This is a very powerful bond in healthy relationships.

The second requirement to quickly writing off debt is to remember that every person is doing the best that he or she can see to do at the moment.

This may sound absurd to many people. "How could you say my ex-wife was doing the best she could when she ran off with the next door neighbor?" or "How can you think that my ex-husband was doing the best he could when he put us into bankruptcy with his drinking and gambling?"

The truth of the matter is no one wakes up in the morning, puts their feet on the floor and says "How can I really screw up my life today?" It just doesn't happen. Sometimes, however, the visible list of options on our menu of alternatives can seem very small. People lose sight of options when they're scared, tired, overwhelmed, filled with self-hatred, participating in an addiction or have limited experience to draw from (such as coming from a household that didn't model productive options).

The disconcerting part of this is that hindsight is always 20/20. We can always see what we (or someone else) could have done. When we berate ourselves for not choosing a different path, we're forgetting we weren't looking at the better choice that we can see now. I hear clients say, "If only I knew then what I know now." I always say, "I'll be first in line when they hand out crystal balls." We would all like to avoid making mistakes.

Try to remember that your partner's choices, and your reactions, were the best you could each see to do at the time. This doesn't mean that you don't have feelings, maybe some strong ones, about those actions, and you have every right to those feelings, to your internal wishes and what you'd like done about the situation. But remember that *internal* emotions and private desires are different from the *external* expectations of what will happen.

Sharing and acknowledging each other's feelings and hopes are important steps in getting through a betrayal, but be detached from an outcome, don't focus on the past. Stay present with what is happening now.

The third thing to remember in "writing off bad debt" in a relationship is that forgiveness is not something you do for the other person. It's a selfish act you do for your own serenity and your own piece of mind.

Often, when we think of forgiveness, we think of letting someone get away with something. Forgiveness is not about ignoring the fact we were hurt. It's not about setting yourself up to get hurt again. Forgiveness doesn't necessarily mean changing your mind. Forgiveness is not something we do to better the life of a partner. It is a very selfish act.

In a strong relationship, being right has to take second place to being serene with one's self. People hold on to "being right" because of fear. These fears are usually never discussed; they just quietly ruin the relationship.

Being afraid that if you forgive they'll just do it again may be very scary. Talk about this fear. It's important to remember that the betrayal probably had nothing to do with you, and whether you forgive your partner or not, it's still 100% up to them whether they commit that action again.

It is disconcerting to realize we have no control over other people's appropriate or inappropriate behavior. Rarely are others conniving and wondering "how can I really upset him/her today?" All sorts of strange and unusual behaviors can come out of stress and anxiety, and they probably have nothing to do with you.

Talk about apprehensions, concerns, and worries with your partner.

You might be surprised at their answer, and be a step closer to a better understanding of the situation.

Be kind to yourself. Long-held resentment can lead to physical symptoms as well; muscle tension, migraines, high blood pressure, poor concentration, sleep and appetite disturbances, and a suppressed immune system, to name a few.

Forgiving is not endorsing what the offender did, or pretending that consequences aren't deserved, but in forgiving we value our peace of mind above all else.

Therapists have a name for that couple that stays together by fighting. We call them "The Bickersons." In one way, bitterness is as bonding an emotion as love. The intensity of focus and connection are similar to couples who obsess about all the adorable qualities of someone they love. Anger may be uncomfortable but it's impossible to completely disconnect from someone when you're filled with hate. Forgiveness frees up all that passionate energy to go into dreams, goals, children, relationships, or a new career.

Forgiveness is a decision we make to enhance the quality of our own life. Forgiveness is not moving our boundaries and allowing the offender to continue to hurt us. We must still respectfully, assertively and with dignity, set our own boundaries and care for our emotional and physical safety.

For instance, if you've been in a physically abusive relationship and your partner refuses to get treatment or work on anger management skills, forgiveness means "releasing from debt," not moving back in or taking the restraining order off. It means not obsessing on what you're "owed," or bringing up how horribly you were treated. It means not seeing yourself as a victim and admiring the parts of yourself that kept you going. It means giving yourself credit for who you've become for having gone through that experience. It means forgiving yourself for being in the situation. After you've been kind to yourself for a while, you'll have the compassion to begin forgiving others.

Once you've decided that your resentment is harming you (and having absolutely no impact on the behavior of your partner) there are strategies to begin putting it down.

Forgiveness is a process. It isn't an event. It is impossible to say, "I'm going to just forget this betrayal and now. What's for dinner?" If you've been ruminating, carrying around bitterness, and watching for opportunities to "cash in" on the debt it may take some time and concentrated effort to get to a place of forgiveness. Having an attitude of forgiveness is one of the most empowering facets of a great relationship.

I've heard Gay and Kathlyn Hendricks speak at their lectures about the power of saying "I forgive you" as often as one would say "I love you." It's part of their daily dialogue as a couple. It doesn't mean being one-down, it doesn't even insinuate guilt or shame. It's simply a comment that if you're in a long-term relationship there will be disappointments and betrayals. They've incorporated this in their normal conversation as a way to clear the tension with this simple phrase.

To start to forgive think about breaking it down into steps.

1. The first take a break and stop obsessing about the betrayal. It's amazing how much time, energy and money people will spend ruminating and planning retaliation. Taking a break can bring a sense of relief and clear your head. Find other things to think about for a while. This will give you a wider perspective when you come back to the hurt feelings and disappointment.

A good way to do this is when thoughts of resentment come to mind say "next," and refuse to dwell on your bitterness. Acknowledge the thought, and then let it pass on through your mind without feeding it.

You won't attract kind, loving people if you live in rage and resentment. Usually you'll just find other angry bitter people, because "misery loves company."

2. Next stop muttering, gossiping or doing hostile things. Just try to refrain from retaliating. You may have to catch yourself halfway through grouchy remarks and just stop talking. It can seem reasonable to withdraw and refuse to cooperate with the offender, but the effort this takes will drain you, not them. Be honest with yourself: Are you trying to make them pay? If so, you're using the wrong tools for your relationship.

Writing down how you feel and what you might want *right now* may be helpful, but you still may need to vent or just be heard.

If this is the case, make sure you ask respectfully "Are you in a place you can listen to me vent? I'm not expecting you to fix or be responsible for my feelings, but I'd like to say some things out loud."

Your partner might say, "No, I just can't listen to any more right now." Ask if he or she would be willing to read about how you are feeling *right now* and what you want *right now.* If they're open to the idea, write them a letter.

It can be difficult to stay present focused when your mind wonders back to a painful event you would like to be different, however, the power is only in the present moment. Communicating is something you can do now.

Gossiping and telling friends and family about what your partner did or did not do is another form of "collecting" on a debt. More about this later.

3. Next make an agreement with yourself to not dwell on the betrayal. This is not to have a blank memory, but to have the person and events move to the back, rather than stay in the front, of your mind. Consciously distract yourself when you start ruminating about the person. Don't live in self-pity. People lose a great deal of creativity, aliveness and closeness by feeling sorry for themselves. Notice where you feel lucky. This can be difficult if you've focused on all the places you feel "unlucky." Practice makes a new habit. Self-care, like sleeping well, exercising and eating health food, is only possible when we move the betrayal to the background.

4. Next, write off the debt. Forgiveness is not giving up and surrendering. It's a conscious decision to stop nurturing resentment and give up get even. It means not educating the other and saving them from making the same mistake again. It means giving them back control over their own life and decisions. We may really think we know what's best for them, but ultimately they're responsible for their own behavior, and forgiving themselves. We're responsible for our behavior, our serenity and forgiving ourselves.

To write off the debt takes a lot of generosity. It takes self-love and knowing that you're whole and complete without ever having things be fair. To forgive the debt means you're not diminished by the actions of the other. You're powerful and lovable even without the repayment of this debt.

5. A final stage is to give up the right to ever hold the betrayal over the other's head. Give up your right to ever bring up the subject again as a weapon. This completely frees you from the hold of grudges and resentment.

The highest stage of forgiveness, and one that's not always available, is to give compassionate assistance to the person who betrayed you. This doesn't mean placing yourself in physical or emotional danger. Nor does it mean forcing yourself on another person, or giving past your point of resentment (co-dependency). What it does mean, is that given an opportunity to provide help, you do so without judgment and with kindness, remembering the strong, centered person you've become.

You can do this by journaling, writing letters you never send, meditating, therapy, praying, walking in nature, participating in group support, talking with a friend, reading books or listening to inspirational lectures. Even if you've never considered yourself a forgiving person, you can begin changing that self-definition today. Life is filled with many unexpected twists and turns.

We cannot do enough, know enough or have enough to keep ourselves protected from all of life's challenging lessons. I once heard motivational speaker, Les Brown say, that we're always just coming out of a crisis, or are in the middle of some crisis, or there's one brewing just over the horizon.

None of us are immune to the disappointments that life brings. Being accepting and fully present when someone is struggling with a life challenge is the greatest gift we can give them. Most people long to connect with a special partner. Even the most cynical chose that viewpoint as a protection against being disappointed. In Aesop's fable, "The Fox and the Grapes," the disappointment is called, "Sour Grapes." These ideas protect our psyche so we can still pursue other endeavors in life with hopefulness and anticipation.

Forgiveness is an art. It's something we practice daily, from forgiving the driver that cut in front of us to making peace with the injustices inflicted on us by well-meaning, but uninformed, parents. Making a commitment to ourselves to practice forgiveness is one of the most powerful ways to bring peace and tranquility into our lives.

Exercises:
Write a list of all the people you need to
forgive, including yourself.

Write a list of all the betrayals your partner has "inflicted" on you.
Write a list of all the ways your anger and
resentment is causing you pain (physical, emotional,
spiritual, economic, social, familial, etc.)
What is the first betrayal you'd like to learn to forgive?
Write a paragraph outlining the specific steps you're committed
to take to start the forgiveness process with this first betrayal.

Board Room:
"Anyone would feel the way I do after what you've done."
"I don't know anyone who doesn't think you aren't a jerk!"
"You broke my trust. You have to prove
to me I can trust you again!"
"If you'd just stop feeling so sorry for yourself---"

Bedroom:
"I'm in so much pain right now. I'm not sure if I can talk to you
a lot without saying it's all your fault. I don't feel responsible
for how I feel right now. I want to take some time to think and
I'd like to spend time with people who will help me find ways
of taking care of my pain without telling you to fix it for me."
"I feel hurt. I'm committed to working on this
relationship. I hope eventually we'll use this
experience to feel closer than we ever have."
"You seem disappointed. I want you to be able to
tell me if you feel bad about something."
"I'm feeling overwhelmed and defensive. I'd like it if
we could both sit and write a list of possible solutions.
I want to feel connected to you as we resolve this."

Chapter Twenty

I is bad for selling. You is bad for connecting.

At seventeen I found myself attending college in Monterey at the first public school I'd ever attended. No longer having financial support I found two part time jobs to work around my academic schedule. One was a small snack shop inside the souvenir store that was attached to a large Japanese restaurant upstairs. On my first day of work the smiling Japanese lady who sold the chachkies pulled a frozen box out of the freezer. I wasn't worried, I knew vegetables and ice cream came that way. As she pulled a cardboard tab and out popped a purplish frozen brick. I took a step back. "Unclean," I thought and then reached out to help. She ran the squid under tap water and showed me how to cut them into rings and batter them.

I'd never seen any meat up close, much less touched it. No one I knew ate meat. It hadn't been served at home, at any of my schools, friend's birthday parties, summer camps, church retreats or potlucks, but I was determined to keep this job. I learned how to make beef and chicken kabobs, and to my relief, fried artichoke hearts. Along with my initiation into foods The World ate, she also told me what to say to customers.

"Are you enjoying your vacation?" "What would you like?" "Yes, you'd like that." "Would you like anything else?" And to the locals who hung out on Fisher Man's Warf, "Did you beat your friends at Bacci Ball?" "What did you catch today?" She taught me how to use "You" in selling.

Effective selling is based on helping your customer, rather than focusing on the sale you want to make. In sales, using the word "you" helps a customer feel that your attention is on their needs, not on yours. Making a customer the center of a conversation with "you" statements increases the chance of closing a deal.

124

Many sales people must use the sales pitch to get the client to choose them over a competitor. Filling the conversation with "you" statements focuses on the client's needs, and how the product or service being presented will make things, better, easier or faster for the client.

Explaining to a customer "Why *you*---" should buy, change brands or reorder, is an efficient way to make a sale.

Elevator pitches are sales training 101. They're brief descriptions of you or your business. The best pitches are focused on the listener's needs and what the company can do for "you."

Relationship building statements are structured around "I" statements. They're focus is self-revealing, not blaming. "I feel," and "I'd really like," are more connecting ways to communicate than "You should," "You always," "You need to," or "You make me feel."

Sentences that begin with "You" in primary relationships, are most likely about to deteriorate into blame, demands or criticism. "You look nice tonight" is not as powerful as "I really like how you look tonight." The first compliment is not vulnerable. It insinuats something is externally true, and takes no personal responsibility for the evaluation. The second sentence is an example of a partner who's participating in the conversation. They're sharing an evaluation they've arrived at inside themselves. It's more endearing. It's more personal. It's more connecting.

During sales calls sellers are instructed to never hang up first. Waiting for the client to disconnect first is an advantage to sellers. In business it's important to make the most of every opportunity. In relationships it's more important to be willing to initiate a time out in an argument.

"I need to take a break here" is better than "You aren't making any sense." When you disconnect from a disagreement make sure you give a reconnecting time over your shoulder on the way out.

Tell your partner when you'll come back and readdress the topic. Demonstrate that you're not disconnecting for good. You're not punishing them by walking away, and you're committed to work on the issue again in the near future. You just need a time to calm down and collect your thoughts so you don't say anything you'll regret.

Many people in business believe that good communication is explaining the logic or benefits to convince someone that a product, idea or service makes sense. "You would benefit," "You should change your mind," "You'll like this." Facts and statistics make sales stronger.

Manipulating your partner with logic and explanations is emotional abuse. Defending yourself with facts and "proof" is joining in the emotionally unsafe conversation. Sharing what you'd like and vulnerably asking for it (insinuating "no" will be an accepted answer, of course) creates connection and trust.

When you use "I" statements, make sure they reflect your emotions or your wishes. "I feel lonely" or "I'd like for us to go on more walks." You partner will care more about what you say in an honest disclosure than all the logical explanations and substantiating facts in the world.

Don't make your partner guess how you feel or what you truly desire. State these directly. Own them. Share them respectfully.

A partner that understands the value of one word in a conversation wrote:

Depending on the moment,
I can be in charge
Or not.
Depending on the day,
I can follow
The Leader
Or not.

I can applaud you feeling good
About yourself
About our relationship
About the world
Or
I can change our connection
With just
The snap of a finger,
The right word
Carefully chosen
Or
The wrong word
Accidentally spoken.
Both satisfy
Depending on the moment,
But let me find more joy
In lifting you up
From where you are,
Regardless of the
Moment.

Exercises:

Notice how you use "I" and "you" in your conversations. Pay
attention to when you're trying to get the listener to change
their mind and when you're just sharing something personal.

Board Room:
"You're supposed to take care of me!"
"You should think this is important too!"
"What do you care?"
"You just decide. You don't care what I want anyway!"
"If you just looked at it differently, you wouldn't feel so bad."

Bedroom:
"I'm scared. I'm afraid that I'm not special and important
to you. Would now be a good time to talk about this?"

"It's hard for me to see you in so much pain. I really wish I could just tell you what to do and make it all better. I believe in you, and I know you'll come out of this successful."
"I feel sad and distant. I don't like it when you're upset. I don't understand exactly why you're angry, and I'm really interested in hearing more about it."

Written exercise:
Write a note to your partner about a feeling you had as a teenager. Write about what you would've wanted at that challenging time of your life. Ask them to share back in writing a feeling and dream they had in high school.

Chapter Twenty-One

If I'm Not Getting Them to Change, What am I doing?

"In life, you have to take the pace that love goes. You don't force it. You just don't force love, you don't force falling in love, you don't force being in love—you just become. I don't know how to say that in English, but you just feel it. When you feel good with somebody, you don't have to force saying something or doing something, if you're just getting to know that person." Juan Pablo Galavis

Many things in life are non-linear. I remember when I founded "The New Mother Counseling Center," in 1990 I made a commitment to myself that I would speak wherever invited to talk on the topic of Postpartum Depression. I received a call from a mom's group out in Harbor City (about an hour's drive from my center, two hours if there's LA traffic). I received a lot of flak for saying I would go. "It's too far, no one with a baby is going to drive all that way for therapy." "It too small of a group, leverage your time better," etc. But I was committed and packed up four brochures and four sets of hand outs and drove to their evening meeting in the dark. I was welcomed into the small house where four women were sitting on a hardwood floor with pillows nursing babies.

I gave my talk, answered questions and headed back to Orange County. I didn't think much about it until I a reporter from the Los Angeles Times called me for an interview. She told me the local chapter president of International Caesarian Awareness Network had referred her to me for an interview on baby blues. I had no idea one of those moms on the floor was a president of anything.

Six months later the same reporter called me and said she had enjoyed interviewing me and could I help her with an article on marital infidelity. I assured her I had much to say on the topic and she did the interview.

About eight months later my phone rang and it was CNN asking if I could drive to their Los Angeles studio to do a live interview with Dr. Sonya Freeman in New York. Seems they had looked through LA Times archives to find a local psychologist who took the position that marital infidelity was a bad thing, who knew.

I assured them that I thought cheating in relationships wasn't preferable and they told me to be at the studio by 7 AM. I spent the night at a hotel near the studio and arrived early. A cordial receptionist showed me the way back to the studio. In later TV interviews I would learn that the little black box with a monitor on the floor to my left and a camera wasn't the norm for most studios. But this was my first TV interview and I didn't know any differently.

The interview began with Sonya and her New York guest who had just released a book about classifications of affairs. I was asked questions from the New York studio. I had to look straight ahead into the camera and lights while trying not to look down at the monitor to see their reactions to what I said. At the last commercial break, I took a sip of water and asked the cameraman how I was doing. He said, "Must be good, Ted Turner's been in here watching you the whole time."

My first CNN interview came out of keeping my commitment to speaking wherever I was asked to new mothers. It led to interviews with Anderson Cooper, Tom Brokow, Susan Powter, Jerry Springer and many many more. Often the most powerful reactions we create come from small actions based on our commitments.

It's hard to explain this to couples when they're in conflict and just want everything to settle down. I always start by explaining everyone's right to feelings and wants. Then I explain the difference between work dialogue and home communication.

After a couple starts to understand they've been bringing work home, they usually stare for a moment and then ask, "So if talking about facts and evidence creates distance in my relationship, how do I get anything to change?"

I smile and say, "You're more than half way there."

There's a famous story about a seeker of truth who went to visit a wise guru up in the mountains of Tibet. He was so excited when he finally reached his destination, he couldn't keep himself from telling the guru all about what he'd learned on his pilgrimage. The master asked if the young man would like some tea.

When the young man nodded, the guru carefully put down a saucer and then a cup, and lifted a traditional tea pot over them. He quietly poured the steaming tea as the young man continued his story. The tea filled the bottom of the cup, rose to the top, brimmed over the side and filled the saucer under it. The master kept pouring the tea and the saucer also filled, the tea running over the edge, streamed over the wooden table, down the table leg, and onto the dirt floor.

The young man jumped to his feet and yelled, "It's full, it's full! Stop pouring! There's no more room for the cup to hold tea!" To which the guru replied, "Yes, if there's no more room, nothing new can be added." The student understood immediately he had to let go of some of his ideas to make room for new ones. There's no curiosity if someone knows everything.

To make real changes in a relationship that has been plagued with occupational agendas, the couple must first stop bringing business communications home. To make room, discard what doesn't work. You cannot begin new closeness building skills if you're sabotaging them with facts, evidence, history, stories and substantiation.

How do things change in a relationship without focusing on outcome? The answer is easy to give, difficult to implement.

Relationships reside *between* two people. A relationship doesn't have a life of its own, as some people seem to insinuate with questions like "How's your relationship doing?" or "This relationship is bad for me," or "My friends think this is an abusive relationship."

Relationships reside in a context. They're relative to your expectations, where you came from (your last relationship or the family you grew up in) where your partner came from, what you're used to, what your partner is used to, etc. Everything about a relationship *is* contextual.

It's like when you've had your hand in cold water, then when you then put it into warmer water, it may feel very hot It's all relative to where your hand was---and what you became accustomed to whether the new water feels like the correct temperature.

If you left an angry, hostile, controlling relationship, you're going to see your next relationship in comparison to that. If you grew up in a chaotic alcoholic family, you'll be evaluating your current relationship from that context.

The same is true for your partner. If your partner just left a passive, distant relationship or came from a family where no one ever showed physical affection, he/she will be evaluating the relationship form that context. If your partner reaches out and touches your hand in public, you may not notice that anything was actually given to you, because this behavior would come very easily to you. From the context of your partner, this was a vulnerable act and they may have been apprehensive that you might react negatively to displays of affection in public, because of their past experiences.

Many of these contextual comparisons happen instantaneously on a subconscious level, we don't even think about them. We just react and make tiny decisions all the time from the context in which we see things.

A direct request may sound rude or disrespectful from your partner's perspective, based on a relative comparison to his/her experience. You might find it hard to believe what you said could have ruffled any feathers, in fact, you felt what you said was "toned down" compared to your own experience of how people talk to each other. This is one way in which relationships are alive and dynamic.

What this also means is, that what each partner contributes changes the probability of what the other partner will do or say. Relationships are morphing, creative entities. They're not stationary so you can't "spot" a bad one or a good one. If you want something in your relationship to change, the *only* thing you can change is yourself.

We have no power to change others, even though that's what all the evidence, story-telling and statistics are attempting to do. Once we see that, there's actually great potential to facilitate change, none of which has anything at all to do with talking your partner out of how he or she feels or what he or she wants.

Gandhi said, "If we could change ourselves, the tendencies in the world would also change. As a man changes his own nature, so does the attitude of the world change towards him. ... We need not wait to see what others do." I think this is a good summary for creating closer relationships. When we are more serene, more direct, take more responsibility for our own feelings and blame less, changes show up in the external world. When we let go of fear and the need to change others, relationships modify to more loving and caring and less defensive and competitive.

I usually apologize to clients before I use the following analogy. It's not as precise as I'd like, but it's the best I can come up with so far:

Marla is in labor, late stage labor, no medication. She's definitely having painful contractions. Imagine her husband, Joe says, "Darling you look so tired, why don't you just go home for a while and I'll take over here."

We'd all think he was a little delusional and probably send for the white jacket.

Imagine he looks up at the fetal monitor, squints behind his wire rim glasses and says, "Sweetheart, this contraction is nowhere near as strong as your last one. Why are you yelling louder?"

Some woman in the room would likely put Joe in his place, if not Marla after she got through the "nowhere near as strong" contraction.

Then imagine Joe sighs, stands up, straightens his pants and says, "Well, I can see there's nothing for me to do here, so I'm heading down to the cafeteria for the rest of this. Call me when it's over."

Everyone in the room would probably be having not-so-nice thoughts about Joe and his abandonment of his wife and the harrowing event she was facing. The only thing she really needed was for Joe to be nearby, be respectful that she was struggling and give her encouragement.

This example includes three kinds of emotional abuse: trying to fix a partner's pain for them by taking over, trying to make them feel better by pointing to the facts, and distancing by disconnecting. What's required when a partner is in pain is just to be fully present and fully alert, showing that you care and are engaged in their process. Providing this gives your partner the opportunity to give birth to new ideas, new perspectives, new aspects of themselves.

We're stronger when we feel loved during time of pain, even if there's nothing anyone else can do to work through the pain for us. We also feel demeaned if someone gives us a trite, simple answer for the struggle we are up against.

Staying present while not giving evidence why someone you love should feel differently, may be the hardest thing you ever tackle in the communication department. Often our first reaction is to try to get those we love out of pain, but this is a business response. If the customer is unhappy, or sales are down, or the distributor has not delivered, the problem needs to be fixed as soon as possible. The same response in a relationship is likely to create more of the problem that you're trying to fix.

Many couples assume that happiness is the goal of being fully present with your partner. This isn't necessarily so. Being compassionately present doesn't take away the partner's pain. What it does do is create closeness and the knowledge that "no matter what you are going through, I'll be here for you."

Just knowing this special person will be by your side is a comfort they would not otherwise enjoy. This is the goal, not getting them to change.

Pushing a partner to change is usually based on some fear. "If I don't get her to change we'll be broke." "If I don't get him to change his kids will never be close to him." "If I don't get her to change I'll have to listen to her nag me forever." "If I don't get him to change he may kill someone driving." "If I don't get her to change she may die." "If I don't get him to change his mind I'll have to live with his family forever!"

Trying to get someone to change to ease our own fears, rarely works, and most often it backfires. Even if we temporarily succeed, our partner may be distant, angry and resentful. If we don't succeed, now we're holding our partner an emotional hostage for not taking care of our fears.

One of the best ways to overcome a habit of trying to "educate," "enlighten," or "change" a partner is to develop the habit of noticing "what's working?" We're all the interpreters of our environment everyday. When we feel lonely or separate we're likely to notice what's "wrong" or "ought to be different." This places our attention on the "broken part." Creating a cue to remind yourself that there must be some part of the situation that's "working" can go a long way towards changing your negative view. Imagine what a stranger might see of value, if you're too close for gratitude. "What part of this is perfect? How could this fit perfectly into my objective?"

With these questions, we can turn "impossible" situations into the perfect events to further our goals. We all fit "reality" and what's happening into our assumptions and preconceived ideas. We're perpetual interpretation machines without even being aware of it.

I have clients argue that it's self-defeating to ask, "How is my husband coming home late form work 'perfect'?" or "How is her running up the credit card perfect?"

I assure them that they'll soon be able to come up with interpretations like: "I'm glad I'm married to an ambitious man who is dedicated to his job, there's so many people out of work." Or, "I'm glad she likes to do things for other people and is so generous. It's one of the things that first attracted me to her." Or "My wife has come a long way having grown up with that! I'm grateful she isn't carrying on those traits and treating our kids the way she was treated.

Noticing how some part of a challenge is "perfect" doesn't mean you don't still have feelings and wishes about it. You can develop the muscle of noticing how something is good, while being respectful of your feelings and how you wish it was. As mentioned before, we live in an addictive culture, and one facet of addictions is "all or nothing" thinking," that tendency to see everything in terms of black or white. When we make ourselves notice another side of some event we've been judging as bad, we increase the chances of finding a workable solution with a partner.

You may want to practice this with your own "self-talk" before you try applying it to other people. For instance: when you notice you're late, rather than saying all sorts of mean things to yourself, try noticing what's right about the situation. For instance, if you got caught in traffic, try: "I have a little more time to myself in the car and have the opportunity to rehearse what I'm going to say in the meeting," or "I'll get to make an entrance and have the ability to acknowledge everyone." When we can find the opportunity in our own blunders, it's much easier to see what's right about the faults we see in others.

Every coin has two sides here are some examples:

"She's obsessive about organizing, but I never have any trouble finding anything."
"He over-explains things, but I always know where he's coming from."
"He's a slob, so he never complains when I leave dishes in the sink."
"I never have any money, but I know plenty of museums you can visit for free."
"She's overweight and never makes nasty comments about other people's bodies."

Exercise:
Notice when you become attached to changing your partner. Ask yourself what's "perfect" right now about some part of the situation you wish to change.

Board Room:
"If you don't stop smoking you'll die!"
"If you loved me, you'd get me out of this apartment!"
"If we don't have sex soon, I'm getting it somewhere else!"
"Either you quit spending so much money, or the relationship is over!"

Bedroom:
"I'm so happy you see yourself as resilient. I'm scared I won't have a long healthy life with you."
"I really like all the coziness this place has to offer. I bet one day we'll look back at this as 'the good old days.' I can't wait to create a plan with you of how we can buy our own home."
"I feel shut out by you. Are you angry or hurt? I really miss making love to you."

Exercises:

Write a paragraph of statements you'd like to use when you feel compelled to threaten or "push" your partner.
Write a list of all the things you find "wrong" about your relationship or partner.
Beside each item on your list, note at least one way in

which this aspect might have some value or might be a by-product of something that did have some positive value. What is a common criticism you say about yourself? Rewrite the above criticism to include *both* a positive aspect, *and* how you feel and what you want about it.

Chapter Twenty-two

UPPING THE ODDS

"Things which matter most must never be at the mercy of things which matter least."
—Johann Wolfgang von Goethe

I left home early to peruse my dreams, but I wasn't the first to do so, by a long shot, in my family. At sixteen my fourth great-uncle, Ethan "Lewis" Alling, arrived alone in Township Five in the tenth range, of the Connecticut Land Company to survey 400 acres that his family in Connecticut had purchased sight unseen. He became the first settler in a town that would become Twinsburg, Ohio. He eventually became the postmaster, stagecoach operator, merchant and hotel proprietor of the town. As a teenager he saw the opportunities he could create in Ohio that wouldn't have been viable back in Connecticut. Relocating 600 miles away in undeveloped territory was a good strategic move.

Good business minds try to "up the odds" of success by starting businesses where their product or service is unique or in a market that will support their industry. Kick Starter is a good example of an entrepreneurial platform that ups the odds of success by testing the market through asking for investors and sharing the risk.

Creating the best odds possible can make or break a business. Many businesses go out of business before they even get off the ground because they haven't done anything to weigh the odds in their favor.

I often hear in my office: "I don't really want to change him/her, I just want to know how to get him/her to stop (start) doing _____."
"I really don't want him/her to change, just tell me how to make him/her be nice." Both of these statements are trying to change a partner. We seem to have a different category for the, "your own good" changes we want to force on loved ones, because it seems

so caring and loving. It's really codependent and controlling, however. Sometimes when we know a change would really be good for someone we aren't aware that it's still trying to change them. It's a cop-out for being responsible for our own discomfort. What we're really saying is, "Make this easy on me. If you change, I won't have to, and we can be happy."

We all have a picture of how our life partner should behave, look, speak, dress, work, play, entertain us, help, interact at social gatherings, etc. The list is infinite, because in a new setting we run head long into expectations we didn't even know we had until faced with it. There's no way someone can know ahead of time all the hopes they may have of a partner, or the discomfort they may feel in new situations. Since changing ourselves is so much work, not to mention embarrassing stumbling around practicing something new, the obvious solutions is, "You change!"

It takes a lot of practice to accept we cannot change someone else. With this acceptance there may be some sadness. There's a loss when we let go of who we thought our partner would turn into. "What can I do to get him/her to change?" is not quite the right question. "What can I do to change myself?" is a better question.

It's important to remember each person has his/her own agenda, fears, history, anxieties, etc. Each person in a relationship needs to only disclose and be only as vulnerable as he or she feels safe doing. If pushed faster than feels safe, you'll see your partner withdraw and become defensive, even if under the same circumstances you'd find it easy to disclose. Disclosure of wants and feelings is a gift, and this gift is usually only given in an emotionally safe environment.

Producing lots of evidence why the environment is really safe will *not* create an emotionally safe environment. Being non-judging and compassionate will help create an emotionally safe environment. Being fully present and connected in a relationship is providing a safe arena where your partner can step up into his/her highest fulfillment of his/her dream. A healthy partner holds the space for the other. One partner does not do the other's emotional work, point the way, punish if they get off the course, or poke and prod to get them to fulfill their dreams.

If you don't try to push or change your partner's feelings or wants (which you might not understand, or possibly don't even agree with) you've immediately "upped the odds" of a productive conversation.

Another way to "up-the-odds" is to thank your partner when he/she discloses something you know was hard for them to say. For instance, if your partner says, "I'm really angry with you for what you said last night."

Try to hear what they are really saying. Listen for a specific feeling. "Angry" was expressed directly. Your partner was not saying "You made me angry," they were taking responsibility for their own emotions by saying "I'm really angry..."

You might feel defensive and say, "I didn't mean anything by it" (or some version of this), in essence arguing that they've arrived at the wrong feeling. This insinuates you know better than your partner how they should feel. Try to remember when your partner tells you how he/she is feeling inside, this is *always* a gift. Most of us don't go around sharing with strangers our most inner feelings and swings of emotions.

A great response might be: "I'm so glad you're bringing that up. I'm always interested in how you're feeling. It looks like it took courage to bring this up today and not just sweep it under the rug. Thanks for your trust in talking with me."

Okay, so not many people talk *exactly* like that, but even saying one part of that paragraph--rather than a disqualifying statement--will greatly up your odds of having a connecting conversation.

You've probably heard someone say to a partner "I love you when you get so worked up!" While in some cases this may sound insincere or even patronizing, it also (with enough lightness and trust in a relationship) might mean "I love you even when you're mad. I believe this is temporary. We'll get through this and I'm not afraid of your anger and I'm not going to try to talk you out of it." Anything you can say that implies (or directly says) these things will create closeness and intimacy.

After you find the words to be able to say, "I feel angry and what I really want is for you to know how mad I am," or "I feel alone and depressed and I notice I'm wanting you to take care of me," or "I'm fighting the urge to tell you how to run your life, and it's taking all the will-power I can generate, I'm afraid something bad will happen to you, and I don't want that to happen," then you can approach your partner and let him or her know how you feel without using threats and extortion. Let him or her know you're committed to stopping the hostage language, and that you are open to hearing how he or she feels about your past threats.

This is an important part. When someone is scared (which is what happens when someone is threatened) he or she may be reluctant for a while to say out loud how they feel and what they want. Be patient. Demonstrate you're not going to keep using threats or insinuation of threats.

You can "up the odds" of having an intimate conversation with your partner by thanking them and complimenting their expressions of feelings and wants, or by expressing your own wants and feelings, and "not moving" or giving defensive evidence back when the reply is less than accepting. Stay in a place where you're expressing how you feel and what you want.

Stay centered and serene. Having good friends to talk with, exercising, reading or listening to audio books, having a supportive community you spend some time with each week, self-exploration and personal growth can help you increase the chances of connecting and closeness-building conversations. When you feel good about yourself, you'll be less defensive when your partner is angry and you'll be better able to stay present with your own feelings and wants.

This may sound easy, but few of us were raised with these ideas. How many of us heard "You can't be hungry, you just ate!" (i.e., you don't have a right to feel hungry or want food). "You can't be cold, you have two sweaters on!" (i.e., you have arrived at a wrong feeling) or "You want to do what? What if all your friends jumped off a cliff would you follow them?" (i.e., you need better evidence to want something.)

Be kind to yourself as you practice these new ways of communicating. You will forget. If your partner is practicing with you, they'll also forget. It's alright to talk about where you messed up later, even a week later. Send a text, an email, a Facebook message. Say "I wish I'd said ---." "I wanted to ask you how you felt." "I forgot to ask what you wanted." It may seem awkward to pick an uncomfortable conversation back up, but you may be surprised by your partner's response.

Words matter. Notice how you feel when you read this poem.

The place we create
For us
Is a safe room.
Protection from things
Outside
But
It's also a place
That protects us
From each other.
We can visit
Together.
Be stronger
Together.
The broken record of
Recrimination

Self-doubt
Mistrust
Fear
Is tossed in the dustbin.
We make our own music.
Lilting.
Evocative.
Uplifting.
Personal
For us.

Exercises:
Notice what you really want for your relationship.

Board Room:
"You make me so mad!"
"You obviously don't care about me."
"You wouldn't do that if you loved me."
"No one else feels the way you do."
"Haven't you been sad long enough? Get over it!"
"Don't worry about what other people think. You
shouldn't feel bad if they don't like you."

Bedroom:
"I'm scared I'm not special and important to you."
"How do you feel about this? What do you want about this?"
"I get so scared when you drink too much. I keep
thinking about my father, the alcoholic. I really
don't want anything bad to happen to us."
"I feel really shut off from you. Are you angry?"

Exercise:
Write a list of three "upping the odds" statements you
could make when your partner is upset or angry.
Write a list of feelings that are difficult for you to
share appropriately (Either you are too silent and
"pretend" nothing is wrong, or you are aggressive
and blaming in your expression of them).

144

Chapter Twenty-three

Your Relationship is not Scalable

"A start up is a temporary organization designed to search for a repeatable and scalable business model" Steve Blank

"Having someone wonder where you are when you don't come home at night is a very old human need." Margaret Mead

"But he's now got the house, the pool he wanted, the country club membership and a new Tesla," my client with the perfect hair complained. Her eyes bounced between me and her phone. She seemed to be adept at texting and talking at the same time. Her apologies always included the amount of money that was at stake if she didn't respond right away. The crumpled top half of a straw wrapper lay next to her sweating Starbucks Frappuccino. Her bouncing Jimmy Choo said this was far from her first caffeine of the day.

"Maybe," I leaned forward in my chair, "he just wants some of your undivided attention."

"So he can just ask me to buy him something else?" She stared at her tapping thumbs, her cheeks flushing, "I don't deny him anything!"

I waited while she put her phone away in a bag the shape of a briefcase, and left lipstick on the straw of her drink.

"All those things may be what he's settling for," I said. "You can never get enough of what you don't really want."

My client and her husband were both lonely. Most people wouldn't notice it in them; they didn't identify it in themselves. The idea that "They have everything they could want, so they should be happy," is based on an assumption that a happy relationship can be set up to be scalable, needing less attention and expecting more satisfaction.

An innovative owner outsources repetitious jobs and delegates the day to day operations to officers, boards and management in a scalable business. A scalable business is expected to grow substantially without continued effort and investment on the part of the proprietor. Good business models are based on sustaining customers and profit. Great business models are set up to create exponential growth without a corresponding increase of effort by the owners. Google, Amazon, and financial institutions are examples of scalable models.

Self-Op businesses like car washes, laundry mats, vending machines and rental properties have owners who are hands-off with the everyday routine operations, as well. These businesses are set up to run by themselves. Even if there's a problem, it's likely outsourced to another business specializing in the issue, such as, maintenance crews, equipment distributors, property managers and attorneys.

We all would like to put in the effort to wash the car, pick up dry cleaning, clean the gutters, wash clothes, and then never have to repeat this tedious task. It's a fantasy shared by all humans: We want something to go on and on without us having to expend energy.

Almost every business owner has considered--maybe on a ski lift somewhere with a view to forever---what it would be like to sell franchises of their bread and butter maker. Everyone who has ever paid their startup fees to join the downline of a multi-level marketing enterprise has had a glimpse of making money from a perpetual money maker while having others do the grunt work.

We've become accustomed to thinking that if something is set up right it will require little or no energy from us. We get irritated when our cable company reminds us this is a fantasy.

While it may be a legitimate goal of business to see how fast you can get out of the daily grind of running the company, and still have it make money, a hands-off approach to relationships only creates a sense of distance and lack of intimacy. No alive, vivacious relationship runs on autopilot. It may be a sign of a successful business to be self-contained and growing while you are away, but it is not a sign of a successful relationship to have no distress or never discuss unattainable wishes.

It may be a cliché, but relationships take work. They take time. They take vulnerability. They take creating novelty. They take contributing new and exciting things you've learned about yourself. They take embracing the uncomfortable and unfixable emotions and situations and weaving safety and closeness out of them.

When we ask a stranger how they are, we're not asking for them to share their deepest hopes and most painful feelings. We expect a polite "Fine. Thank you," and leave it at that. This courteous conversation is appropriate for strangers and acquaintances, but exchanging superficial and stale chatter can be a cop out.

Without doing the work of discovering how you feel and digging within yourself to find ways to describe that, a loved one can be left feeling empty and isolated. Put the work into sharing your vulnerable self. It's hard, but when someone we love trusts us enough to disclose vulnerably what's not going so well, we feel special and needed. We feel like they let us into a part of their life where others are not always included. (Even those who may sound like perpetual victims are probably complaining about the same old things because they believe no one would really care about their deeper fears and pain.)

Being authentic and sharing what's honestly going on with your partner creates a strong connection. We all have the ability to hide out in what's socially acceptable. Most people in relationships have had the experience of a partner picking up the phone in the middle of a heated argument and say in a cheery voice, "Hello!" Hiding what's real may be appropriate and easier when interacting with associates, but it will strangle your primary relationship. Do the work of connecting. Every day.

Let's discuss
The reality of
Unreal expectations.
Specifically
The Belief that
Once a Relationship is
Built,
It never needs
Maintenance.
It's like the Blind Watchmaker Theory
That God created the world
And then walked away to let it
Run itself.
While I can sometimes
Identify
With God's mic drop
And the Desire to get lost,
No one wins in that philosophy.
We're constantly
Mopping up
After unexpected glitches.
Relationships are like that.
Needing care
Pruning
Nurturing
Sustenance
Attention.

Exercise: Notice when you take short cuts in conversations with your partner. What are you detouring around?

Board Room:
"I'm exhausted! Why would you ask me to do that?"
"We always go there. What's wrong with that?"

"I work and pay the bills. That's how I show I care."
"I don't like talking about all that psychobabble stuff."

Bedroom:
 "I wish I had better coping skills to just
let things roll off my back."
"Can I text you my thoughts later? I want to tell you, but I'm
drawing a blank right now."
"Can we take a walk? I miss having time with you."
"I am really upset right now. I want you to listen. I would
really like it if we could turn off the TV and talk."

Written Exercises:

Write a list of things you think you shouldn't have
to discuss or ask for from you partner.
Write how the conversation about those things could create
closeness and intimacy. (Hint: You first have to get out
of, "If he/she *really* cared, I wouldn't *have* to ask.")
Write one way you wish your relationship was on "auto-pilot."
Write about your sadness, agitation and irritation about this.
Write one thing you'll do to let your partner off the
hook from your expectation that they'll (take out
the trash, text back quickly, fill the car with gas,
remember important dates, etc.) automatically.

Chapter Twenty-four

"But I Snoped it, and they're dead wrong..."

"This empire, unlike any other in the history of the world, has been built primarily through economic manipulation, through cheating, through fraud, through seducing people into our way of life, through the economic hit men. I was very much a part of that." John Perkins, *Confessions of an Economic Hit Man*

"Peace cannot be kept by force; it can only be achieved by understanding." Albert Einstein

I grew up in a household that valued debate and winning through evidence. My father's only extracurricular activity in college was his beloved debate team. My parents welcomed the Jehovah Witnesses and Mormon missionaries in for the afternoon with a cup of Ovaltine. My father disciplined me like Voltaire who was raised by his uncle who wouldn't punish him if he could give logical explanations for his actions. Every idea, hope, emotion, opinion had to be backed up with verifiable facts.

Of course my parents' religion was based on facts that went awry. Using bible passages in Daniel and Revelations, William Miller, a Baptist farmer calculated that the end of the world would happen on the Spring Equinox of 1843. When nothing out of the ordinary happened except the days becoming longer than the nights, he changed the date to the Spring equinox of the next year, based on some recalculations of the same facts. When nothing happened again, the facts were read to mean the Jewish Day of Atonement in September 1844. When the wicked weren't destroyed as predicted, the facts were revised to prove that the real day of Atonement was October 22, 1844.

100,000 followers gave away belongings and property. They were certain they were going to ascend up through the clouds to get their reward. There were a lot of upset people.

A woman, Ellen Harman, later to marry James White, came up with a new version of the facts based on the same calculations. She claimed the first angel's message (based on an interpretation of Revelations) was fulfilled by so many people believing the end was at hand. The second angel's message was fulfilled by so many Millerites being disappointed and joining her Advent movement. And the third angel's message, based on the same facts mind you, was that probation had closed and no one else could be saved. Obviously that wasn't a good business model to grow a new religion, so based on the same facts the third angel's message was reinterpreted to mean they had to worship on Saturdays.

On another continent, a Mennonite, Klaas Epp, wrote *The Unsealed Prophecy of the Prophet Daniel and the Meaning of the Revelation of Jesus Christ in 1877.* By 1879, he was preaching that the world would end and his congregation should sell their possessions and move to Turkestan.

After convincing his congregation that the end was very near he founded a village, Ak Metchet, in the domain of the khan of Khiva in October 1882. He finally gave the date he calculated from the books of Daniel and Revelations. When March 8 1889, the proven date came, Epp said as their leader, he would ascend first. So he sat on a church alter, moved outdoors, as a throne throughout the day. They all dressed in white robes and fasted and prayed waiting for the end of the world. When nothing happened he had a great story about how the hands of his ship's clock were hanging at an angle so when straightened, what looked like 8 and 9, was really 9 and 1, so the new date, based on the facts, as he interpreted them, was 1891.

There are many stories of groups deciding an end of the world date based on interpretations of Daniel and Revelations. The Adventists continue to hold annual revival meetings based on the prophesies of these two books of the bible. And many religious organizations point to biblical facts to back their teachings. Pointing to facts is a good way to sell people things to lower their fear.

Many of the clients I see were raised in some version of my debate-'til-you-conquer household. Many of them use these childhood skills to make good livings as attorneys, negotiators or win top sales positions.

There are many areas of your life where fact verification is essential: Airline schedules and destinations, auto repair, medical tests, building plans, to name just a few. This is probably the biggest difference between a business focus and a personal one. Most couples talk about what they meant to say, their real intentions, and how they feel, the same way they speak about their address, the date they got married, and where they last went on vacation. Everything discussed is treated like a fact that could be researched on Snopes or justified by a Gallop poll.

There's no way to prove your intention or give concrete evidence to substantiate that you meant or felt something different. When couples argue, "You know what I meant," or "I *know* how you feel!" they are using the wrong measuring tape.

Applying evidence to tell someone you know more about how they feel and what they want, than they do, is the emotional equivalent of rape. When one person insists they know what the other's internal state is, or should be, they're being disrespectful and intrusive. Even if they're right---however right they could be, since ambivalence is the natural state of humans---defensiveness and hostility are probable responses. We all feel many things at the same time. It's impossible to have only one emotion or only one desire at a time. We are conflicted and responding to many thoughts at any time.

Arguing about the "facts" is generally a waste of energy and builds the walls higher already separating partners. Defending "facts" to the bitter end (sometimes creating sleep deprivation) comes from not accepting the other's right to arbitrarily feel how they feel.

Feelings, hopes, interpretations, blind spots, and preferences are all parts of individuality. No two people will ever experience these things the same way. Trying to talk a partner out of what they want or how they feel, is usually a copout, so that the arguing partner won't have to take responsibility and risk the other one feeling disappointed. Saying no to things that don't feel right is always each individual's responsibility.

For instance, Amanda and Bruce are quarreling about whether or not he has taken out the trash in the last month. He gives examples of several times he's sure he has. She, on the other hand, details accounts of all the times she has given up on him doing so, and has taken the trash out herself. The fight grows more intense, reaching back several years to other trash disputes, and branches out to doing dishes and yard work. Each has evidence and even quote testimonials they recall of friends who have made comments to how much they did in relation to their spouse, and the debate escalates.

What can't be proven by facts and eye witnesses, are how Amanda *feels* (unappreciated, exhausted, etc.) and what she *wants* (help with the trash, to feel supported, etc.)

Bruce can't prove he *feels* "attacked and defensive" and what he *wants* is "to be asked as a partner with respect and gratitude." They're trying to get the other to guess and accommodate them with stories and facts. Then, when no one is guessing right, the flinging of facts becomes more and more disrespectful.

Keeping a conversation present-focused and stating how you feel and what you want *right now* is essential in productive relationship conversation. Drifting into the past is too easy. In the midst of a heated debate, it seems that past evidence *should* convince the other how we feel and what we want. We feel like we must prove we have a legitimate right to these or we'll let the other talk us out of them.

Amanda might have said, "I'd like you to take out the trash right now." A

Bruce could have replied, "I really don't want to right now."

If Amanda's first thought is, "I've been at the office all day, and I took out the trash yesterday! How dare he not want to take it out!" then she's likely to respond with an evidence-based conversation trying to talk him out of what he wants.

If Amanda notices that Bruce has the right to feel however he feels, she's more likely to say something respectful, because she's seeing him as a partner, not a subordinate. "I know you don't want to take it out. It probably doesn't want to go out, either, but would you be willing to take it, anyway? I'd really appreciate it, dear."

Bruce could still decide not to take out the trash and say something sharp like "No, I'm not taking it out. I don't care how much you'd appreciate it."

In which case, from the outside looking in, we can see that there is most likely some other agenda going on. Amanda, if she remembers partnership is not an employer/employee relationship could ask, "You seem really agitated. How are you doing? Is there something you'd like from me?"

If Bruce remembers that vulnerable self-revealing is how to reconnect, he might say, "I've had it with Bob at work. All I want to do is sit and vege-out. Would it be okay if I took the trash out after we ate?"

Self-disclosure is personal, not about observable facts. Now that he's shared what he's feeling with Amanda, she can be there for him. She can't fix it, can't give Bruce more patience, get him a new job, fire Bob, or change Bob's personality, but it matters to Bruce that she cares and that she sees the emotional pain he's in.

This may all sound very melodramatic. It isn't. This process can be used with insignificant, barely noticeable issues to huge "could-end-a-relationship-over-this-one" problems. It's not the size of the issue being debated; it's about not trying to prove feelings and desires (which are always true, but not observable, facts).

Be kind to yourself. You always have a right to your perspectives and interpretations and so does your partner. We have a right to our internal selves. Anything we are sure and confident about, we don't need to defend.

For instance, if you're checking out at the supermarket and the cashier calls you a "Pink Camry," you probably wouldn't be defensive. It's unlikely you'd feel the need to defend yourself with facts: "I don't have a steering wheel!" "I don't have four tires!" "Look, I don't even have windshield wipers!" Because you're secure that you're a human and not a car, you wouldn't waste a lot of time and energy trying to change the person's mind with facts. You'd probably be thinking of reasons they were acting strange that didn't have anything to do with you.

Even if your partner is absolutely wrong about something, if all you do is defend and admit evidence, you miss the chance to see how they're responding to their perception of what is going on. We are all interpretation machines. It's the only place feelings can come from. Regardless whether anyone else sees some event the way you do, you still have corresponding internal feelings and wants based on your own perception, not someone else's.

When we're curious, rather than fixing our partner's internal state, even when they're uncomfortable, then and only then do we get to see what strangers and acquaintances never witness. We get to see their vulnerability and personal self-revelation.

Many of my patients have been emotionally harmed in the past for their vulnerability. They are hesitant to share uncomfortable feelings or wishes that don't match up to the facts as other people see them. For these wounded people, it's even more important that partners and potential partners don't insist that reported feelings and desires be backed by facts. These people (both men and women) need to know that when they share a feeling or want (however seemingly insignificant or large) that it will be accepted.

There's a strong desire in us to not let loved ones get disappointed, as though we actually had any control over such things! It's important to remember that most people are well aware when they're hoping for something that's difficult to attain or unlikely. We can all want to win the lottery, but we know the likelihood of such an event is slim. We can all feel sad or happy at a movie and know it isn't real.

The facts, as an outsider sees them are not good indicators of how people feel and what they want inside. Ask them, with respect, in a safe, non-judgmental environment, and you'll get a much better idea of what's really going on inside them.

The ability to resolve issues doesn't even seem to be reliable in determining if couples will stay together. Dr. John M. Gottman found that up to 69% of the significant issues couples face may never be resolved, but that the couples that stay together (vs. the ones who don't) use coping skills to talk about these difficult issues in ways that made the relationship stronger. (Gottman and Levenson 1976) The couples who split talked in ways that were destructive to the partnership, with criticism, contempt, stonewalling, and defensiveness. Many issues in relationships are not fixable: religious differences, illnesses, in-laws, career choices and their consequences, kids, personal history, or addiction. The things that matter are being able to be responsible for your own feelings by having coping skills to calm oneself, Speaking respectfully with curiosity and being able to listen to your partner's feelings and wishes and then being able to make compromises that don't infringe on either's integrity.

Exercise: Notice when you hesitate to ask for what you want or indicate how you feel because you don't think you have a right to. Acknowledge, at least to yourself, that you have a right, even if you can't explain or back it up with facts.

Board Room:
"You shouldn't want anymore. You've got six at home."
"I didn't get upset when you…"
"You didn't feel like that last time!"
"Your mother said you like that."

Bedroom:
"Sounds like this is really hard for you."
"Well, we're all different."
"I'm always here to listen."
"I'd never in a million years go there, but I
can see it's really upsetting to you."

Written Exercises:
Write a paragraph describing what you can do and say to
stay centered and not try to change your partner. (Even
when you're sure it would be for his/her good.)

Write about a time you felt you were responsible
for your partner's feelings of frustration and gave
evidence why they shouldn't feel that way.
Write about a time you defended something you wanted with a
lot of evidence. How could you have asked for what you wanted
more directly?

Chapter Twenty-five

Grief

"The way to love anything is to realize that it may be lost." G. K. Chesterton

"The only way to overcome the grief☐ is to go through it!" Dr. Paul Gitwaza

"The soul grows through subtraction, not addition." Meister Eckhart

Feeling disappointed and agitated about the way we think things should've happened is part of the process of grieving. Going through the stages of grief is essential before we find acceptance.

Grief is usually only discussed in relation to tangible, significant losses---pets, friends, jobs, spouses and valuable belongings--but we all have little, nearly invisible losses all the time. The grief process is the same, on a smaller scale. When we're disappointed, we're grieving a loss, however small. Unresolved grieving, grieving where we don't feel we have a right to be angry or sad, builds and becomes dangerous in relationships. When we deny our own feelings of disappointment, however small the loss may seem to us or others, unresolved grief builds.

People wonder what all the fuss is over expressing feelings. Grief groups emphasize expressing feelings so we feel "seen" and not invisible. Healing happens when we are vulnerable and appropriately express our emotions.

I like to think of grieving emotions as someone's little kid who just needs to be acknowledged and will then go settle down. If you ignore the child pulling on your pant leg trying to get your attention they'll probably get louder and more annoying. If you take a moment and get down to their eye level and listen for two minutes to their story, they'll probably be off and distracted by something else in the next minute.

Grieving our own emotions is much like that. If ignored and pushed down, they fester. If we say to ourselves "that's a stupid thing to feel bad about, no one else would worry about a thing like that," then the grieving goes into a pot that simmers and amplifies other unacknowledged losses.

When a partner has a "bigger" or "different" dream (want) than what is possible at the moment, there are two primary ways their significant other may react. The first is to explain why what they want is not possible, and hope they won't blame them after they understanding why it's not going to happen.

The second is approach the disappointed partner with an intent to have them feel special, and like a trusted confidant. If someone gives their partner the benefit of the doubt, they can stay present and comfort the grieving partner. This is the "child-birth coach" perspective we talked about earlier: That special person whose presence itself comforts us, even if they can't do anything specific about what we're grieving.

We have a lot of role models for the first way of reacting. Just watch sitcoms or movies, where well-meaning facts and logic are aimed at a lost expectation or disappointment to prove it's too ridiculous, too farfetched, and the person grieving should just get over it.

We have very few models of the second way of responding. It doesn't feel natural to have someone we love who is showing disappointment and just stand idly by watching their distress. Our loving instinct is to point out how they should be realistic, get a grip, and come to terms with reality. They should change their wishes and expectations, get out of their discomfort.

The reality is that only by being fully present with them as they grieve, can you create a sense of unconditional acceptance. Sharing the unmet dreams, the lost hopes, and the process that one goes through to find acceptance *is* an essential way of communicating in healthy relationships.

In business, indications of loss may need immediate attention and repair. In relationships, signs of disappointment or loss may mean they need to be addressed. More often than not though, they're requests to not be alone while the person works though the grief.

Life provides many opportunities to share our losses, large and small. Trusting your partner to be respectful of your grieving process is safety at its best. Love is the ability to work through disappointments and grief, and then celebrate when we get to acceptance and resolution.

Exercise: Pay attention to your own reactions when you feel disappointed or like you lost out on something.

Board Room:
"You're making a big deal out of this. It's nothing."
"You could stop doing that if you just tried. I did."
"What are you upset about? I've always been like this."
"Why are you surprised? Your brother always acts like that at the holidays."

Bedroom:
"You seem so sad. Do you want to talk?"
"I can see you're disappointed. Can you tell me what you were hoping for?"
"I know no one can fix this, but I keep finding myself trying. I'm getting there. I'll remember one of these days."

Written Exercises:
Write a list of all the losses you can think of since you were a child (tangible and intangible.). Take some time to do this. It may take a couple days to think of all of the ones you want to acknowledge.

Write about something you're disappointed about in your relationship.

Write a sentence for each stage of grieving this disappointment:
1. Denial 2. Bargaining 3. Anger 4. Sadness 5. Acceptance.

Chapter Twenty-six

No Long Term Relationship Lease Agreements

"Start where you are. Use what you have. Do what you can."
Arthur Ashe

Romance can be consuming, especially for the young. The adrenalin, the promises of forever and the despondency of loss. We all still remember our first heart break. We were so sure this was the one.

My second great grandmother on my mother's side, Frances Myers, was the daughter of a painter who was in his sixties when she was born in Mansfield, Ohio. He died before she was out of grade school. She knew death was unfair. She'd already lost an older brother before her father. At thirteen, her mother remarried. It was the same year Mansfield's papers covered the mysterious murder of eight-year-old Penny Guinness left cold in her bed for days.

And to add insult to injury, Frances's new stepfather a dentist, came with young step siblings. As a grieving angry teenager she was incorrigible. She was not just sharing her mother with one brother, but seven strange kids and three more to follow in the next few years.

Buying groceries for her large family at the docks of the Mohican River (part of the watershed of the Mississippi) she met a gorgeous and charming mulatto man. The intriguing world traveler, Captain Marshall, erased the monotony of childcare and household chores with his adoration and stories of his ship's voyages to Alaska. Smitten with tales of igloos and polar bears and deeply in love, she ran away and they eloped.

When her mother, Lucy Alling Myers, the daughter of Ethan

Alling, found out, she was furious but patient. When her new son-in-law was at sea in the summer, she rounded up a lodge of local Masons and knocked on her daughter's door. The furious mother and the indignant Masons ordered the distraught bride to file for divorce, come straight home to help with the eleven other kids or be cut out of the Alling family and fortune.

She was heartbroken and even as an old woman she repeated stories of her romantic first husband to her granddaughter and great granddaughter. With a faraway look she fondly recalled how he placed a wind-up music box under their bed whenever he wanted to make love. However, she never did disclose what she did on her annual month-long solo trips to Alaska for the rest of her life.

Years after the shotgun divorce, at 29, a suitable spouse was found, her cousin's business partner who was four years younger than her. They had a prosperous life together raising two daughters. She painted oil paintings (many canvases of snow-covered mountains in Alaska) and collected European paintings that made her feel close to her father. She was so concerned that her daughters would be forced to make choices against their will that she made sure they were financially taken care of. Both my grandmother and her sister lived on the dividends and stock from the Olive Myers manufacturing company.

Grieving is part of life. Finding ways to accept life on life's terms is a difficult task. Some losses are tangible, like the loss of a father or brother. Some are intangible like a mother's attention or the dreams of a young woman.

In a work environment many things can be implemented to decrease the possibility of loss. Insurance, legal contracts, written agreements, laws and ordinances all assist in minimizing loss to a business.

Reviewing agreements is important in a business. Updating legally binding contracts keeps them current and effective. In relationships, there are no written agreements about division of labor or handling emotions. Couples, without giving it a thought, settle in to a comfortable way of doing things. This exchange of support and mutual concern often goes on without a discussion for years. Then, seemingly, out of the blue, the rules change.

If one partner's parents die, the last kid leaves for college, there's a financial loss or gain, a mental illness hits, an addiction hits a breaking point, a hidden resentment boils over, something changes and everything is affected. When the unspoken agreements change in a relationship, both partners may feel the loss of how things have always been.

Even if you've made spoken agreements in your partnership, if you stay together long enough the rules will change. The person who did most of the driving may lose their vision as you grow old together; the person who made the most money may lose their job or a lawsuit; the one who was the most physically fit may fight a life-threatening illness; the one who had the most ambivalence about the relationship may now feel the neediest. Life changes and healthy relationships face the loss, acknowledge sadness or feelings of helplessness and grow with life's changes.

If one partner is doing something because that's how it's always been done in *their* family or insists, the other do something "because you *used* to do it," there will be trouble. Insisting on anything, annihilates partnership and introduces a fear which some relationships never recover from.

If you're not feeling special and important, talk about this, not about past contracts and agreements. The point of power is always in the moment, not in coming to some mutual agreement about the past. Bringing up the past is one of the slipperiest ways to avoid taking responsibility for your feelings. It's also a deflection to try to get one or both partners distracted from what needs to be discussed right now.

If one or both partners try to get things back the way they were, they can't move forward. Change is difficult and stressful. None of us like reevaluating what works and what doesn't in a relationship, but there are ways of navigating these changes that will create more closeness in the end. Much is dependent on our own reactions.

We all would like life to be predictable. The truth is that life isn't. Our best predictions are how we trust ourselves to respond.

My father used to tell me this story:

A family pulled up to the ranger kiosk at the entrance of a national park. The father, his elbow on the open windowsill of their Oldsmobile station wagon, asked the park ranger, "What's this camp ground like?"

The ranger, noticing their bug-splattered windshield, asked, "Where have you just come from?" and handed them a map through the window.

The man behind the steering wheel said, "From that national park up the highway, about 60 miles east."

"Oh yes, Ten Rivers Preserve," the ranger said, "How were the facilities there?"

"Oh, the restrooms were filthy," the driver complained. "The campsites were poorly maintained and the other campers made a racket all night long."

"Well, that's interesting," said the ranger. "That's exactly how it is here, too."

Grumbling, the family drove on into the park and the next car in line pulled up to the kiosk.

The exact same exchange took place, and the ranger asked, "How where the facilities there?"

The driver of the next car replied, "Oh, it was

amazing. The restrooms all had hot showers, the campsites were well marked and the other campers were so friendly we made a lot of new friends."

"Well, that's interesting," said the ranger. "That's exactly how it is here, too."

The park ranger was wise enough to know that the vacationers brought their attitudes with them wherever they went.

Staying aware of changing agreements and your expectations may be the best thing to ever happen to your relationship. Find out where your partner is afraid to share completely in the relationship and how they feel about things are changing, can create closeness. This information is far more useful than "Why don't you do_____ anymore?"

Exercise:
Think about what traits in you have become more pronounced over time. How would you like your partner to talk about and accept these?

Board Room:
"We always go to my family's house for Fourth of July!"
"Why do you think I'll keep picking up your socks?"
"You've never cared about what was in our savings before. Why do you care now?"
"I wasn't raised like that."

Bedroom:
"I'm scared if you change your schedule there won't be time for us."
"I'm confused. How do you honestly feel about going to my parents' home?"
"I feel left out. I want to feel like your partner. Would you be willing to share our financial information with me? I also want to hear about any fears this brings up for you."

Written Exercises:

List at least two things you believed were "understood" at the beginning of your relationship, later to find out these unspoken rules have changed in the mind of your partner.
List at least two assumptions or beliefs your partner felt were unspoken agreements, later to find these had changed or were re-clarified.
Write a paragraph describing the emotional environment you grew up in. How is your current relationship different? How is it similar?

Chapter Twenty-seven

Returns on Investments

"Some of the biggest challenges in relationships come from the fact that most people enter a relationship in order to get something: they're trying to find someone who's going to make them feel good. In reality, the only way a relationship will last is if you see your relationship as a place that you go to give, and not a place that you go to take." Anthony Robbins

Anyone with a marketing background knows that an ROI (return on investment) is how advertising campaigns are evaluated. Most ROIs are calculated by dollars. For every dollar spent, how many were brought back into the business in the form of new business as a direct result of that ad campaign? So an ad that cost $500.00 to run and brought in $2000.00 worth of business would have a 1:4 ROI.

New businesses sometimes overlook this equation and just hope for the best via branding or establishing name recognition. Enthusiastic new business owners can optimistically pour all their upstart funds into PR, advertising and getting the word out. They aren't keeping an eye on their ROI. What outgoing resources are bringing back in is an essential statistic.

Keeping track of what you contribute to your relationship then comparing what your partner does for you is a great way to devastate a loving connection.

People in old photos rarely smiled. But all the photos of my great grandmother show her scowling, if not outright sneering. Marie Sadie Krause was raised the well-established, affluent Mennonite colony in Hutchinson, Kansas. A day before she turned 16 she married Jacob Nachtigall, a new immigrant from Russia. The dreamy teenage girl believed if she left the comforts of her home town they'd become prominent by settling new colonies. They had their first son in the new, rustic colony in Shelly, Oklahoma. Disgusted with conditions in Shelly, she moved back home at eighteen to have their second son. Her parents sent her packing with an infant and a toddler to back to the village in Oklahoma. She bore their next three children in rustic Oklahoma colonies. None of her dreams of becoming famous were coming true. Jacob promised they could still make a name for themselves by moving to an upstart colony in Escondido California.

They packed up five young children and moved across the country to start a farm in San Diego County. A few months after my grandfather was born, her father died back in Kansas. Isolated from her family and unable to attend her father's funeral she focused her rage at the unfairness of it all on the new baby. My grandfather left home at fourteen and found a job in the oil fields in Southern California. His back carried scars from her beatings all his life.

Marie Sadie had two more babies before the Escondido colony failed. Humiliated by the failed community she begrudgingly moved to Shafter with Jacob's family where she had another daughter. She temporarily talked Jacob into moving back to Oklahoma with their ten year-old to try again. Disappointed and resentful for all she'd given up, she returned with her husband to Safter where they both died. She attained prominence. Her resentment, permanent scowl and brutality to her children have been her legacy.

Expectation for sacrifice is looking for ROI in a relationship. This is a calculation for disaster. If one or both partners in a relationship are hoping to get more out of the relationship than they put in, there's bound to be conflict. Contributing energy, time, and money, must come from one's own integrity.

Ask yourself if a contribution (taking off work early, paying for a vacation, or making a complicated dinner) is in your self-definition (i.e., does it match who you say that you are?) If the contribution is not part of your integrity, reconsider it carefully. If you're giving with the expectation that you've purchased the right to get something in return, it's a business transaction.

If you're giving from your authentic self, your contribution will be an expression of who you are, not what you expect in return. If you're withholding of your authentic self from your relationship, you'll unconsciously believe that your partner is withholding their authentic self as well. Even if we're not aware of it, how we walk in the world is how we automatically believe others walk.

Playing full out in life and in your relationship is an act of self-respect. Living in a way that's congruent with your integrity is something only you can be responsible for. If you base how invested you are in your relationship on how much you think your partner is invested, you're no longer in touch with your own integrity.

When a partner wants to be sure they're getting more than they're putting out, they're working from a paradigm that will have disastrous results. In a healthy relationship, the contribution is not 50/50 it's 100/100.

Each person is 100% responsible for their own happiness, serenity and living up to their highest integrity. This may sound disconnected and separate; in actuality, it's the only way two people can be emotionally safe in a relationship, and not make the other one responsible for their happiness and feeling whole.

Only when each person is responsible for their happiness can both partners be able to be fully present when the other is in pain. If the person you depend on for your identity, security, lovability and acceptability is angry with you, you're in danger, focused on wanting to settle them down, and have them get over it so that you can feel safe again.

Keeping track that more is coming in that going out is essential in running a business. Being responsible for contributing what you are comfortable contributing is your responsibility in a relationship. Healthy relationships, with emotional safety, give both partners the desire to contribute all they can.

In business, very little is contributed without some expectation of return. Even if that return is establishing a business contact or a tax write-off. A good business person watches for the opportunity in everything. "How can I get a return on this?" "How can I write this off?" "Who in this room could help me further my business?"

The object of a healthy relationship is a place where you get to give love, a place to recharge your batteries, to grow, and to be revitalized towards your life's purpose. Another person cannot give you happiness or a feeling of self-worth and value. These are things individuals must find on their own.

Having a fulfilled life, where you wake up excited and energized every morning, is one of the best gifts you can give to your relationship. There's no return on your investment that will do this internal work for you. We all have to do it for ourselves. Give from a place of self-knowledge, not expecting increased returns, and you will find the ROI of satisfaction and peace inside yourself.

Exercises:
Remember what you were told by your parents about what to expect in a spouse. Do you have different ideas?

Board Room:
"I have worked 12 hours. You have a flexible
schedule. You've got to do it."
"I do everything around here! You don't do anything!"
"I've earned sitting and having a beer! Leave me alone!"
"What did you do all day?"

Bedroom:
"I'm exhausted. How are you feeling?"
"I'd love to go out to eat. What do you feel like?"
"I'm tired. I'd love to go take a bath. How would you
feel about watching the kids for a half hour?"

Written Exercises:

Where do you feel taken advantage of?
Where do you get scared and may not keep your own boundaries?
When was the last time you thought "My
stress is far greater than his/hers"?
Write about what you see is in your own self-definition as
a partner. (Hint: What do you need to do to feel good about
yourself as a good partner, but won't build resentment?)

Chapter Twenty-eight

Sold Out To Buy the Farm

"Lots of people want to ride with you in the limo, but what you want is someone who will take the bus with you when the limo breaks down." Oprah Winfrey

Many couples are still happy after they've achieved their financial dreams together. Many of them have grown closer over the years dealing with the reversals of fortune, investment challenges, occupational changes and raising difficult children together. Many are still the team that created their mutual goals.

However, I often hear a patient reminisce about how it was "back then," when they didn't own a house and were sewing curtains for the apartment windows and eating fast food to save money. The simple times are remembered with tenderness. Many times happiness and financial success are inversely correlated for couples, especially if the price they paid for financial security was ignoring the vulnerable connections that keep couples feeling close.

It's not financial success itself that creates the distance. Many couples respectfully divide up childcare, house hold tasks, work, financial obligations, bill paying, scheduling, holiday tasks and the numerous other activities that make a home. But for many couples the outcome-focused conversations take over the ones that bring them together. Before the pressing obligations and busy schedules they took time to focus on the moment and share their dreams and the things they felt.

As a business mentality takes up more and more of the conversation---"The mortgage is due." "We need to set up college funds for the kids." "Did you pay the plumber?" "We need a new car," more and more intimacy is lost.

There are a neurological changes with the habits we develop. What we do over and over creates stronger neuropathways (tiny active, chemical/electrical synaptic highways) in our brains. The habit of talking about what needs to be done and who will do it, overrides the ones that used to make us laugh and feel like best friends.

To weaken the business-focused habits and develop new routines requires practicing clumsy, not-so-polished skills over and over, until the new neuropathways are large enough to compete with the previous ones.

New habits are not easy to develop and ones that make us feel vulnerable (like learning new communication tools) are even more challenging. We like being competent. Our business mentality tells us that the more competent we are, the better and that if we don't know what we're doing it isn't good to show it. If you're determined to look good and protect yourself from feeling vulnerable, you will probably never acquire the communication tools to create emotional intimacy.

To practice being self-revealing and vulnerable in front of the person who knows you best is a daunting task. If you decide to stop applying business rules to your relationship and place closeness and intimacy higher in your priorities, give yourselves a lot of credit. Most people settle and keep running like a rat on a wheel, hoping that with enough facts and enough convincing, they can make their partner reconnect and feel close again. It will never happen.

Just the events of daily life can reinforce a business conversation for couples, and eventually they have lost all remembrance of how to *be*. All they know how to talk about are facts, other people, and storytelling to support their ideas and desires. They've lost all ability to actually self-disclose and reveal what is vulnerably inside them.

I often hear couples complain they have no time to do things together. They once believed they were temporarily trading closeness for financial security, but days turned to weeks, weeks to months and now, years later, they've forgotten how to connect. They long for the days they had leisure time on weekends or date nights. When they had less, they shared dreams with each other and felt safe sharing sadness or excitement.

Life does not require that we practice closeness-building skills. Plenty of people live without them. It's a luxury we actively choose.

Ten steps to simplifying my life:

1) Fewer possessions. If it doesn't give me joy...it's gone!
2) Less time on the Internet.
3) Trim down the Facebook feed.
4) Pack my lunch.
5) Get a bike: More exercise, less gas and insurance.
6) Meditate.
7) Walk two miles every morning.
8) Listen to more Patti Smith.
9) Get up an hour earlier and work on my poetry.
10) Don't say yes to a project, unless I feel passionate about it.

Exercises:
Reminisce with your partner about simple things
you did when you first started dating.

Board Room:
"All you ever think about is money!"
"Why do you have to have everything you see?"
"Talk about feelings? What new self-
help book have you bought now?"
"What do I want? I want you to not bug me
with this wants and feelings stuff."

Bedroom:
"I really like it when we spend alone time together."
"I would really like to make a list with you of all the
things we'd like to see and do before we die."

"When you take so much time out to choose
a present for me, I feel special."
"It's really hard for me to talk about feelings.
I'm not sure I even have the words."

Written Exercises:

Write a list of things you'd like to do to simplify your life.
What's the first thing you'd need to do to
start each of the items on your list?
Write a list of low/no cost activities you'd
like to do with your partner.
Write two of these on the calendar within the next month.

Chapter Twenty-nine

How The Game Is Played

"This dissociation from the body extends to emotional disengagement. Without access to his feelings a man can't help but lose track of who he is, what his priorities are and what is normal for him." Mary Crocker Cook, *Codependency & Men*

My maternal grandfather spent part of his childhood living in a boxcar outside of Houston, Texas. The humiliation motivated him to do anything to become financially secure. After trying his hand at sales he joined the Navy and trained to serve on a submarine. Deciding the submarine assignments weren't for him, he got reassigned to the Navy Midshipman football team. In 1918, coached by Gil Dobie, the Midshipmen compiled a 4-1 record, shut out two opponents and outscored the competition with a compiled score of 283. Due to WWI the traditional Army Navy game was cancelled as the season was cut short.

He learned about competition and winning at any cost. He returned home to live with his parents in Los Angeles until he was 35. During that time, he and his brother ran bootleg whiskey to speakeasies while making the most of relationships with corrupt prosecutors, even judges. He eventually took a job training salesmen for Shell Oil Company to sell refinery by-product gasses for industrial chemicals and catalysts.

Beating the competition by optimizing one's advantage and playing to win are how games and sports are played. Sales competitions for luxury vacations, vying for coveted "C" positions, and going after limited grant funds are all ways businesses minds play the game.

While it may create adrenalin and excitement for a while, that kind of game playing in relationships leads to hostility and retaliation.

So, if winning isn't the game, what is?

"I don't get it," Lillian says. "How do we ever get anything done if I just listen to what he wants and acknowledge how he feels?"

This is the eventual question couples ask when working on their relationship. It can seem like nothing will ever get resolved.

"Think you can better problem solve if you trust each other and give each other the benefit of the doubt?" I ask.

"Sure," she says, "but when does that happen?"

"It's like learning how to do an obstacle course," I say. "You need many skills to keep going in the direction of the finish line. Only focusing on the finish line will stop you cold when you have to swim, jump, swing, run or climb if you don't know how."

"Sounds complicated," Lillian says. "I just want us to get along."

"Relationships are complicated," I say. "You can 'just get along' with a pet. A real relationship requires decision making by two individuals who respect each other as adults. That's not always easy."

"I respect his opinion," she says. "I'm just better at this sort of thing."

"You may be," I tell her, "but what price do you think you'll pay in the long run if you don't listen and acknowledge there's another side of the issues?"

"So now I'm responsible for his resentment?" she snaps.

"You sound defensive," I say. "Are you worried his feelings are your responsibility?"

"I want us to stop fighting and going over the same issues over and over. I think we're both resentful."

"So when you hit the part of the obstacle course that requires skills for resentment, or confusion or defensiveness," I say, "you need tools to reconnect and create emotional safety so you can keep heading toward the goal."

"So it's like recalibrating?" Lillian says.

"Something like that," I say. "When you've re-established that you've got each other's back, you'll both see many more possible solutions."

"So it's about finding more possible resolutions before getting to a final resolution," she says.

"Two heads are better than one," I say, "and when there's no anxiety shutting down the higher functions of both brains, it's not just better, it's creative and inspired."

"So we do get to some decision?" Lillian asks.

"Anytime you push to get to a conclusion--ignoring that you both have feelings and wishes about the subject--you're in danger of buying frosting for a cake that's burning in the oven." I say. "Make sure you attend to the process of the cake before putting too much emphasis on the frosting.

We are so accustomed to focusing on the outcome of activities that we often don't know how to talk about anything else. When we play a game, we are often competitive and focused on winning. Play has lost its meaning. In its most pure form, play is a non-goal directed activity. When children play, they watch caterpillars crawl. They run and slide on long strips of water covered plastic. They splash and laugh in swimming pools. They play with their food. They're fascinated with the nature of things. This insatiable curiosity and ability to become absorbed in the now is often lost in the serious pursuit of "more responsible" activities. Developing both is the trademark of maturity.

Playing a game of golf is sport. Watching waves break on the shore is "play." Playing a game of cards is competition. Listening to music is "play." Playing a game of basketball is outcome-focused. Watching a sunset is awe-inspiring.

Real play takes us to a place of joy and serenity inside ourselves. Games, on the other hand, are based on competition and beating the other side. Play creates a sense of connecting because there's nothing to be "one up" about. Games and sport, by their very nature, place us in competition "against."

Our culture does not endorse real play very much. I believe this is one of the reasons we have such high incidences of anxiety and depression. All anxiety disorders arise from the fear of the future. Anxiety comes from worrying and anticipating. As you can see, fear (anxiety) is based on focusing on a possible outcome.

This is not to say there's not an important place for outcome-focused activities. It's important in life to have goals and direction and feel a sense of accomplishment for attaining these goals and dreams. However, if outcome is all that a person knows, there is an eternal emptiness with very brief and fleeting moments of serenity when a goal has been met, just before the next goal looms on the horizon. Just watch an infant struggle to crawl, and as soon as that is attained, watch the struggle to scoot along the sofa, looking so proud, but only for a little while. Then the frustration of wanting to walk shows up. When walking is attained, then running as fast as possible and falling down becomes the parents' challenge. Then the frustrated desire to dress him/herself and the echoing "I do it!" is heard ringing through the home.

The desire to accomplish more and have a feeling of greater success is naturally wired in us. For some people, that success means successfully acquiring a skill, such as learning a second, third or fourth language. For some, it's learning a musical instrument. For others, it is educational success. For others, financial success. The definition for each person is different, but whatever someone is after, there's one thing in common with all of these goals: The person has to place one thing arbitrarily ahead of another.

If a student decides getting good grades and getting through school in four years is what he/she wants, then this becomes more important than partying with friends and socializing until 2:00 a.m. every night.

Anything can become a game. All it takes is to make one thing more important than other things. To play the "game" of relationships well, it takes making closeness and process, more important than "being right," "getting one's way," "being understood," "doing it the most expedient way possible," and doing things "because it should...."

These are very difficult concepts for couples to incorporate into their daily life habits. We're all programmed to place the things that are defendable at the top of our list. However, if intimacy and closeness are what you are after, placing connectedness and respect ahead of educating the other is essential.

Let's examine two conversations. The first places being right as the highest goal. The second places being close as the goal.

Russell: "I thought you said you were going to pick up the dry cleaning today. Can't you ever keep your word?"

Tammy: "I told you I would pick it up if I was in that part of town. Why do you always twist my words around?"

Russell: "I need my gray suit for tomorrow's presentation. You don't ever care what's going on in my life. Can't you ever put what's important to me first?"

Tammy: "I put what's important to you first all the time! Where do you think I was all day? I was shopping for your mother's birthday present and getting groceries for your dinner!"

Russell: "It looks like you took a detour to get your nails done and I bet you had lunch with your girlfriends! You are just trying to wiggle out of admitting you lied about not picking up my dry cleaning!"

Tammy: "I didn't lie. I didn't say for sure I would get it. You're always putting words in my mouth and you never care about what I have to say. I do a lot for you. You're just never appreciative. Why should I do any more for you when you don't even appreciate what I am doing?"

The entire conversation was based on facts, not a vulnerable feeling or want statement in the whole exchange. Now a couple who places closeness above being right:

Marlin: "Did you stop and pick up dry cleaning today?"

Alicia: "No. I forgot. Did you need it soon?"

Marlin: "Yes, I have a big presentation tomorrow. I'm sort of nervous about it. I like how I look in my gray suit. I thought I'd feel more confident wearing it."

Alisa: "I'm sorry. I didn't realize it was important to pick up the dry cleaning today. Is there anything else I can do to help you feel more at ease? Would you like to run the main points of your presentation by me?"

Marlin: "I really appreciate your support. I know when I get anxious about work, I expect more from you. Thanks for being there for me."

Alicia: "No problem. I have my moods, too. How about if I leave at 6:55 in the morning and pick up your suit while you're showering?"

The first thing you may notice about this conversation is they both appear to be on the same team. This is what conversation looks like when couples place an emphasis on how they feel and what they want. Both conversations start with problem solving, but in the second conversation fixing the problem was not as important as self-revealing and being curious. This sharing and accepting of each other's wants and feelings *is* what makes problem solving easier. Not finding the right *facts* or being accurate enough.

What you might also notice about this conversation, is that Marlin and Alicia placed being in partnership and feeling close *ahead* of being "one-up" or trying to educate the other about facts. This focus on remaining friends can do a lot for improving conversations between couples.

If the contractor you are working with is not following through on his/her commitments then it is time to find another contractor. However, in relationships, there will always be misunderstandings, differences in priorities, fatigue, distractions, physical illness, etc. The "game," if you will, in relationships, is to place feeling connected and having a best friend, above the myriad of trivial challenges that present themselves in life.

Most of the things we worry about in life never happen. The things people fight about for days, usually have very little to do with any serious consequences. They have just placed "being right" or "being accurate" above being close.

Baz Luhrmann's song, based on an essay by Mary Schmich at the Chicago Tribune, *Everybody's Free (To Wear Sunscreen),* goes, *"The real troubles in your life are apt to be things that never crossed your worried mind, the kind that blindside you at 4pm on some idle Tuesday."*

When these real issues strike, it is important to have a life partner that is on your side and will be your best friend as you both walk through these challenges together. If you have built a relationship on "the evidence" and being right, it's likely you will feel very lonely when these "dark nights of the soul" hit, even if you are surrounded by many people.

You're responsible for the game you decide to play. In your life, in your relationship, what do you want to make more important than something else? All the therapy or self-help books in the world will do no good until you have decided this question.

Is business or work more important than anything else? Is having a warm nurturing relationship more important than anything else? Is proving you are right more important than anything else? Is trying to change someone else more important? Is harmony, or growing old together, most important? Is your contribution on the planet most important?

Only you can decide what game it is that is worth pursuing. Once you decide, take responsibility and play "full-out." Life is short and the time to start living fully is today. Don't put if off until some unknown future date. The game you are now playing is building on itself. Everything you do adds to it.

Exercise:
Pay attention to times you're tempted to show that you're right, even though you know you will be unkind.

Board Room:
"If I don't push you, you won't get anything done!"
"There you go again, only caring about yourself."
"See, this is what I predicted would happen!"
"You just say what you think people want to hear."

Bedroom:
"I'm afraid the things that are important to
me aren't as important to you."
"Even though I know our schedules are busy, I
want you to know I think about you all the time
and carry you with me wherever I am."
"I like that you're so compassionate to other people. I'm afraid

you may let some people run over you and you may get hurt.
I want you to know I'll be here whenever you need me."
"I admire that you're a trial-blazer. I'm excited by your new idea. I also get scared when systems are new and untried."

Written Exercises:
Write about one time in the last month you made
being right more important than being close.

Write about one time in the last month you made
being close more important than being right.

Think of one activity that genuinely could be categorized
as play that you would like to do with your partner.
Put it on the calendar within the next week.

Chapter Thirty

RESPECT

"You can kiss your family and friends good-bye and put miles between you, but at the same time you carry them with you in your heart, your mind, your stomach, because you do not just live in a world but a world lives in you."— Frederick Buechner

My grandmother, Vivian Chapin, was the first woman commercial artist on the West Coast. She had an Orange and black studio in Los Angeles. She painted children's bedroom murals for affluent homes in LA. She did calligraphy for books and products. She drew all the artwork, headings and cover art for *Fashions in Food in Beverly Hills Recipes*, published in 1930 by the Beverly Hills Women's Club. It had an introduction by Will Rogers and recipe contributions by stars like, Mary Pickford, Douglas Fairbanks, Buster Keaton, Joan Crawford, and Fannie Brice.

She did the art deco artwork for Diamond Matches boxes. She worked hard for the respect she earned.

She'd won a full scholarship to the Otis Art Institute when her talent was recognized by teachers at her finishing school, The Bishop's School in La Jolla, California. No one in her family had made a career out of art and certainly no woman had been self-supporting through painting and drawing. Feeling isolated in her second story studio, she found a colleague on the East Coast. She regularly had operators place long distance calls to revitalize her creativity by connecting to a peer. She found ways to nurture her self-respect as well.

Many couples come to therapy focused on respect and how to get more of it from their partner. They believe they can demand or teach their partner how to respect them. They want to instruct their partner to treat them with the respect shown to casual friends out having dinner.

I explain living day in and day out with a partner is more complicated. What most people mean by respect is that intangible kindness we seek behind closed doors when we're not getting what we want and there seems no good reason why we shouldn't get it!

One of the biggest challenges in developing this rare brand of respect is that when we're upset we feel a strange sense of entitlement. We feel justified in being angry, even rude or verbally abusive. Picture returning to the Customer Service desk of a department store with a small appliance---for the sixth time. Think about how your conversation with the customer service representative might go. Cranky, raised voice filled with frustration, demanding satisfaction. Now imagine that a grad student from your local psych department gives you both surveys, rating each other on several scales of politeness or rudeness.

When the grad student scores these questionnaires they're likely to find that both you and the customer service representative have significantly different ways of rating your behavior. The customer service employee, having just got back from lunch break, is frustrated and confused at this irate person interacting with them. You, on the other hand, are back here for the sixth time. You've reboxed the warrantied gadget, fought traffic, hunted for a parking place and hiked through the mall, just to meet with the same script of placating patter!

Your verbal attack seems justified, even necessary to make something significant happen. To the baffled employee, your attack seems unfounded and targeted at the wrong person. Each of you would rate the level of your rage and indignation very differently. This is the same subjective dance when we interact with a life partner.

We bring home all the frustrations we keep hidden out there in the real world. Out where we might have unwanted consequences if we let people know how we really feel. So our pent up frustration ends up getting targeted at the safe person in our life because they'll understand how it is out there, give us the benefit of the doubt, and not retaliate.

I often hear married couples complain, "He/she treats strangers better than me!" Most of the time both partners have participated in this passive-aggressive battle. Sometimes this discrepancy comes from one partner overestimating the emotional connection in the relationship, believing the other partner is so dependent the relationship doesn't have to be nurtured, or their own insecurity that even strangers will see their weaknesses.

Open up conversations about feeling taken for granted or not heard. These conversations can be face to face, over the phone, texted, written in letters or emails. Don't start with long drawn out lectures. Begin with short, curious sentences. Allow time between discussions. Passive aggressive behavior is unconscious by its nature, so it may take time and self-reflection to respond honestly.

Sometimes, in business, a potential customer is temporarily treated better than a significant other. This new customer could walk away, buy elsewhere, talk bad about the company, or help the competition. It's a great investment in your relationship to treat your partner with the respect you would show a valued customer, but it's the nature of business to be professional and to present yourself in a competent manner to build client trust. In your personal relationship vulnerably and honesty build trust. Having all the answers and never showing weakness builds walls and creates distance with a loved one.

In a respectful conversation it's important to let go of your sense of entitlement. Proving that you're smarter, better, more motivated or more sensitive than your partner is extremely dangerous for a relationship. Making someone else wrong and pointing out why you're right, can't create a close loving relationship. In fact, showing contempt in words or actions is one of John Gottman's primary predictors of divorce.

It may take courage to self-reveal and speak about "how you feel" and "what you want" when you're upset with your partner, but to speak down to him or her or make them "wrong" for what's happened, only places a larger wedge between the two of you. Creating a safe environment by self-disclosing, without making them responsible, can be a more rewarding way to communicate.

Remember, respect can only be modeled. You can set a respectful mood for interacting when you feel tension or disappointment, but you cannot control your partner or "enlighten" them. Lecturing someone about how they should be respectful is *not* modeling respect or setting an atmosphere of respect.

Pay attention to how you speak when you're agitated, offended, or disappointed. Don't be accusing. Don't stay silent, hoping your misery will be detected by your significant other. Don't count on them asking what's wrong, letting you off the hook from initiating a difficult conversation. Pay attention when you may be looking for a reason to vent. Be honest with yourself if you're just looking for something to "regain ground" from a previous battle with your partner.

It's always important to take a look at your motives. If you're not clear about your priorities, you're likely to end up playing "I'm right because I have the best evidence." This is a very lonely game to play.

R-E-S-P-E-C-T
Find out what it means to me.
R-E-S-P-E-C-T
Find out what it means to you.
Aretha knew that it could be a
Sock it to me
It couldn't be earned.
Money couldn't really
Buy it.
And that you have to ask for it

More often than
It's
Given.

Exercises:

Watch what you label as "disrespectful." What else could
you say? (Maybe they're tired, had a long day, have a lot on
their mind, didn't understand, aren't feeling well, etc.)

Board Room:
"Do you have any idea how you sound?"
"What are you trying to prove?"
"A lot of good all that self-help stuff is doing you!"
"If you just looked at the facts, you wouldn't feel that way!"

Bedroom:
"I am so afraid that nothing's going to change.
I feel sad and separate from you."
"I'm so angry, I don't even have words to describe
it. On a scale of 1-10, I am a 9.5!"
"I'm so tired of fighting with you. I feel discouraged and
resentful. What I want is to take a break and go for a walk."
"I am committed to you. Even when I'm angry and
hurt, my commitment level is still a 10."

Optional Exercises:

Write a paragraph describing when you feel disrespected.
Write about how you generally try to "educate" your
partner out of being disrespectful. What kinds of things
do you say? Are you insinuating he/she does not have a
right to how he/she feels? How does your voice sound?
Are you calm or agitated? Are you compassionate or
insinuating "wrongness" as you are "educating"?
Write a paragraph describing how you would like to respond
when you feel disrespected. What words would you like to use?
How would you like your voice to sound? How would you like
to convey respectfulness as you discuss your feelings and wants?

Chapter Thirty-one

But They Promised! Can't I Hold Them Accountable?

"Love takes off masks that we fear we cannot live without and know we cannot live within."
— James Baldwin

An employee will have consequences if caught lying, stealing or being dishonest in their job. These consequences may be verbal warnings, being written up, suspension without pay, getting fired or even arrested. All these consequences are to protect the welfare of the business and provide a warning to other employees.

I'm often asked in my practice, "If someone close to me breaks a promise (repeatedly) don't I have the right, if not the duty, to hold them accountable? Is it right for them to just get away with it?"

Feeling as though we've been lied to can create feelings of mistrust faster than almost anything else. The fear that we can't count on our partner is scary. Catching our loved one in a lie can release rage we didn't even know we had.

Feeling deceived can be triggered by a partner failing to keep their word. From not keeping a promise of bringing home milk, to relapsing back into an addiction, to hiding a secret that threatens the integrity of the relationship. All these inconsistencies can create fear and anger.

The question isn't if we have the right, but *how* these issues are discussed. Holding a partner accountable is a very different thing than holding an employee or a team accountable. Taking a broken promise personally, while understandable, shuts down communication and may keep you from really understanding what your partner is thinking or feeling.

If you are attached to your partner "doing the right thing" *whether he/she promised it or not*, you're in a supervisor or boss role, not an intimate companion role, and your relationship will feel the repercussions of your authoritative stand. Even if you're attached to teaching them something that is for their own good!

There are three points I would hope you'd remember when starting conversations about broken promises. First, it is possible your partner changed his or her mind. Saying we changed our mind is something that's not popular in our culture to admit. It is number four, "I have the right to change my mind" of the ten assertive rights in Manuel J. Smith's, *When I Say No, I Feel Guilty: How to Cope Using the Skills of Systematic Assertive Therapy*.

Making it safe in your relationship to say, "I've changed my mind," may be one of the kindest things you ever do for each other. When it's emotionally safe to tell one's truth, even when it may not be the popular response, both partners feel special and important to each other. I encourage partners who may be codependent and worried that they're responsible for making sure their partner behaves right, to regularly review these assertive rights.

Second, lies and deceit are based in fear. If you really want to understand why your partner ducked and covered or was conflict avoidant when being asked to be forthcoming with the truth, ask about fear.

Being afraid causes us to make poor decisions. The fight or flight chemicals that flood the brain when we're frightened make logical, thought out decisions more difficult to access. The emotional parts of the brain are activated and avoiding perceived danger becomes paramount.

When people have conflict avoidance, they've learned that horrible consequences follow when someone is upset with them. This phobia may be learned in childhood or in a previous relationship. Like other phobias, it can't be addressed with harshness or anger. You can't help someone overcome a driving phobia by yelling at them. For example: You can't assist someone who's afraid of elevators by shaming them.

Like other phobias, finding out it is safe to take incremental steps, is the only way out of Conflict Avoidance. Talking about small things their partner may not really want to hear, and finding out the partner is curious, takes responsibility for their own feelings and is not punishing are small steps that help conflict avoidance sufferers. Threatening to leave, scolding, giving the silent treatment or retaliating are like dropping the elevator three floors after the phobic person has progressed to getting in an elevator at all.

If you or your partner avoids telling the whole truth because of conflict avoidance, a therapist may be able to help. Fear is the opposite of love. Don't let fear crowd out the love in your relationship.

Thirdly, if your partner has an addiction, remember the very nature of addiction is denial. *The Guide for the Family of an Alcoholic* provides a succinct letter that the loved one of any addicted person will recognize. The addiction may very well be alcohol, but drugs, gambling, sex or eating disorders can be exchanged for "alcoholic" in this letter. *AN OPEN LETTER FROM AN ALCOHOLIC can be found on Al-anon's website*

An untreated addiction is like an illicit affair. The addiction is the lover, always coming first in the relationship. A partner's decisions, secrets and emotional pain will all center on their addiction. If your partner struggles with addiction there are many ways you can stay centered and respectful by taking responsibility for your own emotions.

Al-Anon groups are for those affected by an alcoholic. S-Anon groups are for partners of sex addicts. Nar-Anon groups are for loved ones of drug addicts. O-Anon is for loved ones of those with eating disorders. CoDa groups can help support those who try too hard to keep their loved ones away from an addiction.

If you're building anger and resentment because your partner doesn't keep their word about an addictive behavior, seek support.

Support groups are available in most communities and online groups are quickly becoming popular.

When a partner doesn't keep a promise, you may feel it's your right to teach them a lesson. Maybe it is, but it will only create more anxiety and distance. The more fear and detachment in your relationship, the more likely your partner will feel afraid to tell you the truth in the future. Shaming, scolding, educating, score-keeping and hostility will not increase the chances of your partner keeping their word to you.

If your partner choses to seek the advice of a professional, a sponsor, clergy or a teacher they're more likely to follow that advice. This doesn't mean you're less important to your partner. You have a much greater presence in your partner's life than any of these other people. They may play only one role in your partner's life and they may even be paid to occupy that one role. It's easier for us humans to take instruction from someone who will not have another agenda or "ulterior motives."

When we ask professionals for advice, we believe they are more detached. What we do with their advice is up to us. The attorney or counselor won't be having coffee in the morning and say, "Well did you---?" Professional detachment *increases* the chances we will act on the advice.

Remember you already add something very important to your partner's life as a support, comfort, sounding board, and confidant. You're the one person in the world your partner knows will be there for them, whether they succeed, fall on their face, go slow, or go fast. Unconditional acceptance doesn't mean you don't have feelings and hopes about your relationship. It does mean you lead with curiosity, giving the benefit of the doubt.

If you feel betrayed or duped, own your feelings. Ask for what you want. Be curious about how your partner feels. Respectfully inquire what they would like from you as you work through the broken promise.

Kelly: But you promised….
Tom: I know I did.
Kelly: I made plans…
Tom: I'm sorry. I …completely forgot about it. I must have gotten distracted.
Kelly: So you weren't thinking of me, just yourself.
Tom: I always think about you! What you think, what you feel, how you'll react, but this time, well….I just have to say no.
Kelly: Who'll call the Bennetts and tell them that you changed your mind?
Tom: I'm happy to call them. I have nothing to hide.
(Long pause.)
Kelly: I'm not happy about this.
Tom: I have the right to change my mind.
Kelly: Not when I make plans.
Tom: Even if we've made plans, I have the right to say no.
Kelly: I would never do that to you. Even if I hate where we're going, I'll do it for you.
Tom: Please don't! You have the right to say no, too.

Exercises:

Notice when you take a broken promise personally ("I must not matter!") Think of three other possible reasons your partner may have not kept their word.

Board Room:
"You said you'd never do *that* again!"
"Of course you have high blood pressure, look how you eat!"
"We'd be so much happier if you only ran your life differently."
"I can tell you anything a therapist could tell you, and I'll tell you for free!"

Bedroom:
"It's hard for me to see you struggle. I want to fix it for you. I want you to know I'll be here to support and encourage you."
"I worry about your health. I want to tell you how to live your

life. I get scared I'm going to have to live without you."
"I'm scared your therapist will tell you bad things
about me and encourage you to see yourself as
a victim. I'm scared my perspective will get left
out. I want you to know I care about you."

Optional Exercises:

Write about one topic in your relationship where you
believe it is easier to lie than it is to tell the truth.
Write about what fears surround this topic for both of you.
Write a paragraph describing how you could talk about
this topic with the focus on "how you feel" and "what you
want" with no evidence, or facts to try to change him/her.
Write a list of things you are afraid will
happen if your partner doesn't change.
Write a letter to your partner---you don't have to give it to
them if you don't want to--- stating that you accept them just
the way they are, and that you are supportive of however
fast or slow they decide to change things in their life.

Chapter Thirty-two

"MEMOS" - GOSSIP

"When you stop expecting people to be perfect, you can like them for who they are."
– Donald Miller, *A Million Miles in a Thousand Years: What I Learned While Editing My Life*

Gossip has been dangerous throughout human history.

My Grandma Lois' mother, Jennie Towne, was a direct descendent of my 9th great-grandfather and great-grandmother, William Towne and, Joanna Blessing once accused of being a witch. They were the parents of Rebecca, Mary, and Sarah Towne, the girls accused of witchcraft in Salem Village, Massachusetts and artistically portrayed in Arthur Millar's play, *The Crucible.*

Rebecca, a 71-year-old grandmother, denied an attorney, was hanged in Massachusetts in 1692. Mary was released from jail and then rearrested on the gossip of another spiteful woman. Mary was found guilty and hung two months after Rebecca along with seven others. While waiting execution she wrote several petitions regarding changes in trial proceedings, how witness and defendants were questioned and the representation of accused witches.

Sarah, my 9th great aunt, escaped execution and was released from jail after eight months of imprisonment.

Seventeen years after the death of my 9th great-grandfather, Deacon Samuel Chapin, who served as a Magistrate in Massachusetts, petty resentment and vicious gossip brought three innocent upstanding women to trial. Two died in humiliation public hangings in front of their children and grandchildren.

We may think that because we have fewer superstitions or that consequences won't be so severe that gossip about loved ones is benign. It isn't.

In an office, it's important to get news out about things that need fixing. "The copier in the mailroom is out of service." "The front stairwell will be closed for painting." "The water will be turned off from 2:00-3:00 by maintenance." "Parking lot B will be painted on Friday." These are important pieces of information that need to be distributed in a business. They're true, useful pieces of information that may or may not affect all employees, yet the memos are distributed office wide.

In a relationship however, when there are things that are not going so well or may seem to be in need of fixing, sending out memos to everyone is not a good idea. It can be very tempting to tell friends and family about how unfair he/she was, how much money they spent, how he/she is "back at it" or how he/she will "never learn." This venting to friends and family can soon be gossiping. Gathering a sympathy squad does nothing to better your relationship. In fact, you may be reluctant later to tell these same people that things are getting better.

This is a difficult area for many couples. There is usually one partner who needs more social support than the other, and who is more likely to seek out someone to "vent" to. The other partner feels betrayed and may even be embarrassed to see their partner's confidant at a social or family gathering.

Sending out memos and telling everyone in your close circle that there are problems, is not appropriate. Having a couple of close friends, a therapist, clergy, an objective relative, a 12-step sponsor, or a support group with a confidentiality agreement, are appropriate places to process your feelings and wants. Be very thoughtful before you decide to complain about your partner. It's usually more productive if you focus on how you're coping and how you can take care of yourself.

Friends are likely to agree with you that if only they changed, your life would be wonderful. Educated and trained professionals are more likely to ask, "What are you doing to keep yourself centered?" or "Do you know how you feel and what you want?"

If you're complaining that your life partner isn't matching the picture you had in your head, and you're sending out memos complaining to anyone who will listen, you're bringing a hostile person into your relationship. You're saying that you're not willing to look at anyone but your partner as the source of conflict and that changing their behavior is the only answer to your misery.

Well-meaning friends and family can actually amplify relationship issues. Even if they don't join you in putting down the behavior of your significant other, they may blame you for your bad choices.

To wallow in self-pity is disrespectful of yourself. Even bemoaning that you've "chosen poorly again" is to see yourself as a victim and belittle yourself. Even if you find yourself in a similar condition, the truth is it's impossible to create an exact situation over and over. Each time you're faced with a complicated event in life, you have the opportunity to learn something new about yourself, your coping skills, fears or desires. You can never go into a similar situation again, without having the past information you've learned.

This is important, because many people, when they begin to take responsibility for their lives, start by blaming themselves. They say, "I'll never learn. They've done it to me, again. I should've seen it coming." This self-berating is *not* taking personal responsibility. Don't let friends and family convince you that your significant other is 100% to blame, or that you are, either. Don't get caught up in these over simplifications. They can distract you from what really matters. No relationship is all bad or all good.

Relationship is a process. It's an active, alive, dynamic, ever-changing progression. It's only as *real* as two people decide to make it. If you need to talk to someone about issues in your relationship, remember that a relationship resides *between* two people. It's not a free floating entity in and of itself. Your input is every bit as impactful on the relationship as is that of your partner's. You're an active participant. Even refusing to speak directly to your partner is contributing something to your relationship. Something that's likely to create more distance and discomfort, but it's still an important contribution.

If you decide to talk with someone about difficulties in your relationship, make sure you're choosing someone to talk to who will direct you back to what you can do. You only have power over yourself, today, and what you choose to contribute. The only person you can ever change is yourself. Period.

You'll take a big step toward bettering your relationship if you make a commitment to only speak about your discomfort with those who'll hold you accountable. Helpful support people will see you as powerful in your own life. They'll view you with compassion and yet remind you that you have it within you to create an incredible life. They'll see your current situation as transitory and see you as the powerful creative person you are.

Share with those who will help you keep your commitments to yourself: Your commitment to speak up sooner so you don't build resentment; your commitment to surround yourself by other people who support you for following your dreams; your commitment to exercise or use other ways of reducing stress; your commitment to feeding yourself. If you've made these commitments to yourself, keep them.

Remember, if you gossip you're also changing the perception of those around you and your partner. If you're committed to your relationship, stay aware of this potential fallout when the two of you are patching things up. It's not easy to stop gossiping, whining or focusing on "making them pay." Journaling can help when you feel like you're going to explode if you don't put words to your thoughts and feelings. There are professionals, therapists, clergy and support groups where "getting it off your chest" will not come back to affect your partner.

Remember that what you give energy to "grows." You'll get more of whatever it is you think about, talk about and focus on. If you're focusing only on the parts of your relationship that aren't working, it will be much more difficult to grow the parts that are successful.

Janet: So you talked with Phil about what was going on with you and me?
Bryan: I was feeling lonely and depressed about it. He's my best friend. I had to talk with someone!
Janet: I'm so embarrassed that other people know about our problems! What did you tell him?
Bryan: I'm not comfortable rehashing the conversation.
Janet: It was that bad?
Bryan: It wasn't anything you and I haven't already talked about. I felt that going round and round about it with you hurt us, instead of helping. Phil was a safe place to turn to.
Janet: It feels awful to think that I'm not a safe place for you.
Bryan: You are. I just wanted a change of perspective.
Janet: What did he say?
Bryan: He was helpful. Phil played devil's advocate a lot, so that I had to ask myself tough questions. He pushed me to consider you more and not just make it about me.
Janet: I'm happy to hear that.
Bryan: He suggested that after I got stuff off my chest with him, that I come back and work things out with you.
Janet: How do you feel now?
Bryan: I look at things differently. I'm still unsure how to solve the problem, but it doesn't seem as overwhelming as before.

Exercises:
If you have a habit of complaining and gossiping to others, write a list of options you can do instead. Remember it's important to acknowledge your feelings, but how you do this is a choice. Give yourself credit when you notice yourself holding back from participating in these behaviors. Compliment yourself when you ask directly for what you want from your partner and when you focus on the positives in your relationship.

Board Room:
"Can you believe he's still doing that! When will he ever learn?"

"I don't think she'll ever change. She's always
been like that, always will be."
"If only she'd realize money doesn't grow on trees,
then I'd start treating her with respect."
"If only we could go out in public and he wouldn't
embarrass me, then I'd start to respect him."

Bedroom:
"I believe we can work things out. We've
been through difficult times before."
"I want you to know I believe in you. Even though things are
difficult and I feel confused. I'm glad we're talking about this."
"I wish you wouldn't talk to the neighbors about our
issues. I want you to feel safe enough to talk with me about
them. I feel embarrassed when I don't know what they
know. I feel scared we won't work on our problems."

Optional Exercises:

With whom do you like to talk about the
challenges in your relationship?
Is this a safe person? Will they be objective, keep your
confidence, and redirect your attention to what *you* can do?
With whom would you like to talk about
your issues in your relationship?
Write a paragraph you'd like to hear from
someone who you chose to support you.

Chapter Thirty-three

WHO ARE MY COMPETITORS?

"A loving relationship is one in which the loved one is free to be himself — to laugh with me, but never at me; to cry with me, but never because of me; to love life, to love himself, to love being loved. Such a relationship is based upon freedom and can never grow in a jealous heart."
— Leo F. Buscaglia, *Loving Each Other: The Challenge of Human Relationships*

At seventeen I lifted my head up off the hot asphalt of the university library. My ears rang and my vision was blurry. My boyfriend of three and a half years was yelling above me. "You could've written mine too. How long would it have taken you?"

It dawned on me the blow to the back of my head had come from him. I didn't even know we were arguing. I decided that day I needed to get far away. I finished out the semester, but I never again lived in my home town. It took a long time to understand his jealousy of my academic grades had nothing to do with me.

I had heard stories of my grandfather's jealousy of his girlfriends after my grandmother died. He had made many mob connections running bootleg whiskey for a decade of prohibition. In an unusual fatherly gesture, he took my mother to Palm Springs for a vacation. This appeared generous from the dad who refused to pay more than six dollars a month child support. My great-grandmother who was raising his two children couldn't find an attorney to take her case to ask for more, because he had several judges in his pocket and they were afraid of him.

Sitting out by the pool, my mother at ten asked him when they would have to go home. He said he didn't know. Every day he read the Los Angeles newspaper. The day an article appeared describing the assault and broken leg of a man he believed had dated his most recent girlfriend, he said, "okay, I'll take you home now."

Many business coaches, business evaluators or marketing experts will encourage those in business to ask the question, "Who are my competitors?" This helps focus on who else is in your type of business, providing similar products or services to potential customers. For instance, if someone were considering building a hospital or a pizza store they'd want to know, ask "How close is the next hospital?" or "How many pizza stores are within a 5 five-mile radius?"

The question "Who are my competitors?" insinuates there is "only so much," and that a business owner needs to find out who might "take their share." This question implies scarcity. For business investors this is valuable. They want to know what the potential market is for a particular service or product before they commit resources.

This belief in scarcity can also be found in many relationships. Some partners are preoccupied with potential competition, worried that someone else will come along and "steal" their partner. Some people are afraid that their significant other only has *so* much attention to give, and they need to be sure to get "their share." These jealous partners discourage interaction in the very activities that made their loved one interesting to them in the first place. If the targeted partner tries to take responsibility for the jealous one's fears, their circle my become smaller and smaller until they feel trapped and suffocated. People become jealous and fearful for many reasons. Sometimes it's mere projection and a means to keep the other partner off balance so they don't see what's right in front of them. A partner may also feel that they're not good enough for their current partner. They may have been raised in households where one parent cheated on the other, or had partners leave or cheat on them. There is no way to go back in time and change events, but talking about these can create trust. The reasons are less important to talk about in the relationship that the anxiety itself.

Being in a relationship with someone who is insecure and fearful can put undue strain on a relationship. Trying to appease an insecure partner, and mind-read what might set them off, will only provide disastrous results. The anxiety of answering, "Where were you when I called?" or "I thought you were supposed to be home by 6:00," will erode emotional safety and create resentfulness in a relationship.

Jealous partners can escalate around other people or at social gatherings. Biting statements like, "I saw you looking at her!" or, "I saw you flirting with him!" going out with other people will become stressful. Fear rather than love becomes the bond in the relationship. If a partner is going through the other's belongings, always ending conversations with a hint of suspicion or fear, their defensiveness will run the relationship.

Chemicals--marijuana, methamphetamine, cocaine, MDMA, even alcohol--can create a sense of unrest and paranoia in people. If chemicals are involved in the suspiciousness in your relationship, focus on that first. It will be impossible to convince your partner you're trustworthy if their perceptions are clouded by a chemical.

When a partner senses the other is afraid of losing the relationship, and capitalizes on this by making threats to leave if the other doesn't change this or that, the relationship stops being a partnership. Using the threat of abandonment will never create closeness, and sometimes the damage that ensues is irreparable.

Once someone threatens to leave, they can never take the threat back. They may say, "Well, I was just mad, I didn't mean it," but the other will always know that if they get mad again, it is possible they will threaten to leave, again. Trying to strong-arm a partner into changing can take a great deal of time and effort to heal. Threatening to leave a relationship is an immature way of talking about feelings and wants. It's like saying "I'm taking my toys and going home." If someone is feeling; lonely, sad, neglected, or unimportant and what they want is to; be held, have time together, receive phone calls during the day, get a kiss upon leaving and arriving home, make love more often, or feel cherished and important. They are too immature to ask for these, so they resort to threats.

This may sound crazy when we're talking about it this way, but many people have a great difficulty discussing their vulnerable feelings and wants, resorting to a corporate threat of, "I'll just take my business elsewhere." This may indeed work for banks, investment houses and restaurants, but is verbally abusive in relationships.

Verbal abuse is similar to physical abuse, in that, once someone has used it as a weapon, their partner can never again interact with them as though they never "went there." Yes, people can overcome verbal and physical abuse in relationships, but the abusive partner must gain better coping skills and learn how to deal with their own fears of not being special and important. The receiver of the abuse must learn how to separate themselves when the abuser is in the one-upmanship mode. It's not possible to de-escalate abuse with logic. Logical arguments with evidence and facts are the fuel that feeds the abuser's fire.

If you or your partner is interacting in your relationship as though you might lose something to someone else, it's important to remember you're in a personal relationship.

Remembering that you're special and that you're enough, is an important step in overcoming a scarcity mentality in your relationship. If you know you're a good catch and know you have value, you'll be better equipped to stay centered if your partner tries to get you to change by threats of leaving. You'll be better equipped to re-focus the conversation back to what they want and how they feel. You'll be able to respect these even if your answer to some of their wants is "no." You'll be able to do this while staying centered and true to yourself.

When someone really understands they're a good catch, they're able to use a sense of humor to help discharge tension with lightness and laughter. This isn't sarcasm, which is one of the most aggressive and hostile types of communication there is, and it's not poking fun. It's seeing the incongruences, looking down the road at how this will look years from now and finding lightness in the moment.

If the threatened partner is unsure of the other's commitment level, the threats to leave will grow to the point where one partner is in control and the other is walking around on eggshells. Any power skew in a relationship will erode sexual desire. When there is no emotional intimacy, physical intimacy will soon be lost.

It's important for each partner in a relationship to know for themselves that they're valuable and worthy. If there's too much self-doubt they'll find themselves hinting at how they feel and what they want, instead of disclosing these important conversations without defensiveness and distracting evidence.

I often hear "I don't want to change them, I just want them to understand." To which I usually answer "*Understanding* is very overrated and making someone understand IS changing them. It's changing their mind.".

You are a unique person with your own strengths and individual challenges. No one is exactly like you. You have no competition for who you are. If your partner is focused on "trading up," they'll have that focus no matter who they're with. Building a long-term relationship with your best friend and partner takes maturity and commitment.

I have told you many times that I'm "outta here" and while I've always come back, I know that threatening to leave doesn't make the situation any better. Instead, it just implies that I'm not as committed to this relationship as I say that I am and that I don't care as much as I feel I do. So, if it's okay with you, I've decided that if the discussion gets heated, I'll walk into the kitchen, get a glass of water and then come back. It's not to run away from what's happening or to take control away from you, but to regain my self-control and continue the conversation. Being gone for a couple of days prevents us from being together to work things out, so I'm not going to make angry threats, anymore, either. I know my behavior puts a barrier between us every time I say those things, that it chips away at the bond that we have. I want a place where we can both say what we need, freely and safely.

Exercises:

Reminisce with your partner about a jealousy early in your relationship. Discuss how you created a deeper commitment to each other by working through it. Share how that experience helped you in the future.

Board Room:
"Are you looking at her?"
"I saw you flirting with the clerk. You think I don't see those things? You think I'm stupid?"
"Where were you all yesterday afternoon?
You didn't answer your phone!"
"That's it. I told you if this happened again, I was out of here!"
"One day you're going to come home and find me gone!"
"Do you think anyone else would put up with you?"

Bedroom:
"I feel scared and unimportant when you look away while I'm talking with you."
"I think that clerk thought you were cute. How do you feel? Can I tell you when I feel insecure when it happens?"
"I get so scared when I don't know where you are. I wish I felt more secure in our relationship. What I want is to be able to ask you for reassurance when I feel afraid."
"I feel us growing farther and farther apart. "How do you feel?" What do you want about this?"

Written Exercises:

Write a list of ways you know you're valuable,
and would be difficult to replace.
If you use threats of ending the relationship as a weapon in fights,
write a paragraph of something else you could say that would
be respectful and acknowledging of how you feel and what
you want, but doesn't use blackmail to get your point across.
Write a paragraph of things you'd like to do or say if
your partner threatens to end the relationship.
Write a list of qualities you see as irreplaceable in your partner.

Chapter Thirty-four

COMPETITION VS. COMPASSION

"When you are content to be simply yourself and don't compare or compete, everybody will respect you." — Lao Tzu

I've hiked down the Grand Canyon seven times, once was from the north rim down to Phantom Ranch and back up the south rim. My father loved hiking. He was never in a hurry. As a kid I spent time identifying animal footprints, collecting colorful pebbles and looking for Indian pottery. My father always carried far too much on his back pack. Extra firewood, water, food and first aid supplies. I was fascinated with the snake bite kit. I never saw him use it, but it always made me feel safe out in the wilderness.

We would watch other hikers jog by seeing how fast they could make it to the bottom and back up. He was always courteous and my brother and I were told to stand to the side of the trail and let the competitive packs go by. They kicked up dust and left waffle stomper prints in the fine clay. About two or three water wells down, inevitably a day hiker would be red and sweating sitting under the wood awning. My father would undo his hip belt, take his Army-issue canteen off his green canvas riveted belt and fish out a bottle of salt tablets. He never gave the heat exhausted hiker just one or two, but a whole bottle. "Don't worry," he'd say, "I've got plenty." We often had heavy accented happy campers around our roaring campfire, as there was no natural wood in the canyon to burn.

My early American Mennonite ancestors were the first organized group to decry slavery in a written statement. It was presented to their Quaker neighbors at a meeting. Sometimes compassion for human beings takes longer than it ought to. Competition can blind people from recognizing it and embracing it as the only answer.

Businesses, even ones that focus on People, Planet and Profit, still need to stay competitive.

Competition is about winning and one-upping an opponent. In a competition, the two (or more) sides consider each other the adversary. In competitions the goal is to do better than the opponent, whether or not it's a personal best. The only focus goal is to beat the other side.

This creates polarity. A dividing and separating of goals happens. You can feel this kind of competitive division if you've ever sat on the wrong side of an important sporting event. Not only are the players focused on winning, but everyone watching feels compelled to take a side.

Competition makes people sharp. They're able to see weaknesses in their opponent and take advantage of these to better their own position. A competitive spirit places beating the other side at the top of the agenda, with all exertions of energy pointed toward that end. Competition creates a single focus of attention.

Compassion, on the other hand is different. The focus of compassion is to "see" the other side. This seeing or understanding, is not to gain an inside advantage, it's to gain a sense of where the other is coming from. Compassion is never about outdoing the other. In fact, it specifically doesn't create opposition. There's no attempt to beat or show the other one up. Compassion is about joining together, rather than dividing to conquer. In compassion there is no single focus, but rather a global, inclusive one that includes other perspectives.

Even when weaknesses are revealed, compassion doesn't use them to take advantage. Self-disclosure of these are viewed as places of vulnerability and tenderness. Courageous self-disclosures are seen as areas of personal growth, healing, and intimate secrets to be treasured and kept safe.

Compassion, while gentle, is a very strong force. Competition may at first seem stronger, but it's only an appearance.

There's an old Native American story about a contest between the wind and the sun to see who was stronger. They decided whoever could get the buffalo skin robe off a strong young warrior would be the winner. The wind was the first to try. He blew and blew as hard as he could, sending gusts and gales of biting cold wind that pulled and tugged at the heavy robe. Small flaps would open up as the wind blew harder attempting to rip the robe off the young man, but he pulled the robe even closer and braced himself against the angry wind.

Then the sun took his turn. He smiled down on the young warrior, warming him with radiant light and surrounding him with sunshine. The joy of the sun kept flowing over the young man and his buffalo hide. The sun continued outpouring his warmth and embraced him with the brightest of light. The warrior relaxed and stopped bracing himself. He let down his defense and a smile stretched across his face. He slowly opened up his robe. Then, taking a deep breath, basking in the warmth of the sun, he threw off the heavy robe.

This is a simple story about the differences between force and warmth. Every culture has stories of how compassion brings greater outcomes than force and competition. Many stories use water as a symbol of compassion. Water is soft, fluid and adaptable, but it's also the most powerful force on our planet.

Some couples believe that sarcasm and bantering are ways of bonding. In some cultures debating and intellectual competition are seen as legitimate terms of endearment. Besides the fact that these are terrible skills to work though the bigger challenges life will bring, the unconscious mind processes belittling and degrading humiliations literally. If we repeatedly hear "You can't do anything right," or "You always mess up," or "See, I have to take care of things, you're incompetent," the mind comes to believe that these are "true," and self-esteem plummets.

This lowered self-esteem may come as a shock to a partner who thought that they were just "messing around." They may defend verbally abusive statements with, "That's how they know I really care about them," "I only tease the people I really love," etc. As resentment, hostility and defensiveness build, a competitive partner may be baffled by the passive-aggressiveness or explosions of anger from the "teased" partner.

I've seen many individuals over the years, who come into my office shocked that their partner finally said, "I'm done. I want a divorce." They had no idea the difficulties were all that bad, but over the years, competition crowded out compassion to the point there was no intimacy left. All the, "I'm only kidding. Where's your sense of humor?" in the world can't create connection and emotional safety.

These disqualifying comments insinuate that "You've arrived at the wrong feeling. You shouldn't feel hurt. You should feel close and safe. What you want is also wrong. You already have a connected relationship." This is the essence of emotional abuse. Partners of people who disqualify uncomfortable feelings and real desires for closeness will feel defensive and often feel guilty for their defensiveness because they don't understand what emotional abuse is. Often these undermining statements remade behind closed doors because friends and family would be able to spot the abuse.

Compassion isn't necessarily something people learned in their childhoods. It can be developed. Compassion is a perspective and commitment, just as competition is a perspective and a commitment. One way to see this difference outside a romantic relationship is to watch a person play games with small children. It quickly becomes apparent if the adult is trying to win or attempting to help build self-confidence in the child.

Those playing with the child to win will worry about cheating and playing right and fair.
They'll focus on strategies and calculate moves to beat their opponent. An adult playing to connect from a place of compassion, will focus more on laughing, teaching a sense of humor and showing

empathy. They'll compliment the child for effort and creativity. They'll notice ways of celebrating a sense of accomplishment and praise the child. They may not necessarily let the child win, real compassion isn't about patronizing, but the focus will be on building them up not running them over.

Developing compassion is one of the most important elements in a healthy relationship. Putting down a competitive stance, and letting go of seeing your partner as your "adversary" is the beginning to closeness.

Remember that COMPASSION has the word PASSION in it. If you want more passion in your relationship add more compassion, and passion will come with it.

Karen: I feel bored. Let's go to Disneyland.
Burt: Right now?
Karen: Sure. Why not?
Burt: What brought this on?
Karen: We've been working a lot, lately, and I want to have a play day with the man I love.
Burt: Is he coming, too?
Karen: Very funny. Do you want to go?
Burt: Can we get cotton candy and buy Mouse ears?
Karen: Whatever you want.
Burt: So what will we do when we get there?
Karen: Be kids for a few hours. Whatever we want.

Exercises:
Stay alert to when you or your partner slip into
a competitive debate. Ask yourself how you
can add compassion to the conversation.

Board room: "You had problems with your father.
That's why you can't get along with me."
"You grew up with nothing, that's why you're so stingy."
"You never did well in school, that's why you have to prove something to everyone now."

"I got this done in half the time it usually takes you."
"Let me do it, I can finish it!"
"I do twice as much around here as you do!"

Bedroom: "I like that you're so compassionate to other people, but I'm afraid you may let some of them run over you. You might get hurt. I want you to know I'll be here whenever you need me."
"I admire that you're a trial-blazer. I'm excited by your new idea. I also get scared when systems are new and untried."
"I admire how far you've come with so little to work with. I feel privileged to be in a relationship with you."
"I really am in awe of your courage and tenacity. I feel lucky to know the parts of you that you don't share with just anyone."
"Would you like me to help? I'd like to. I feel sad when you have so much to do."
"I'd like to just sit. I'd like you to just sit next to me. I miss you. I love you."

Optional Exercises:

Write a paragraph describing what compassion means to you and your relationship.
Write a paragraph describing what competition means to you and your relationship.
Write a paragraph about how you can start demonstrating more compassion for yourself, your own feelings, and wants, *and* those of your partner.)

Chapter Thirty-five

A little Distance Doesn't Mean Death

*"Once the realization is accepted that even between
the closest human beings infinite distances continue, a
wonderful living side by side can grow, if they succeed in
loving the distance between them which makes it possible
for each to see the other whole against the sky."*
— Rainer Maria Rilke

*"True friendship comes when the silence between two people is
comfortable."*
— David Tyson Gentry

I often see a husband or wife in my practice who becomes terrified
when their partner asks to take a break during an argument. Their
fears range from believing it is the end of the relationship to that
they are being punished to they are no longer needed.

Healthy relationships have a flow of close times and times when
there is some space between the individuals in the committed
relationship. The type of distance and length of time differs with
each couple. Some partnerships thrive even though one or both
partners are deployed for months at a time. Other couples just need
a monthly night out with the girls/boys.

No two people have the exact same need for connection and
freedom, so this is territory that needs to be discussed and
sometimes re-discussed over the years.

The need for autonomy is built in to every human. We express it in
toddlerhood when we first say, "Me do it!"

Likewise, we all fear abandonment. The worst punishment handed down in the traditional Mennonite colonies was shunning. When a member of the community broke a law or tradition that was deemed heresy or otherwise dangerous, the rest of the community would act as if that person didn't exist. They didn't speak to them or respond in any way. Most often they were forced to find another place to live and find work.

In prehistoric times being cast out of the clan, away from those circling around the fire, meant sure death by wild animals or marauders. We all have a deep seated anxiety about being thrown away from safety.

At the extreme, is what psychologists call Borderline Personality Disorder. This mental illness is very severe and disrupts sufferers in every area of their lives. They constantly interpret the word and actions of those around them as threats of abandonment. They are very emotionally immature and cannot calm themselves when upset better than a young child could. These people are very difficult to live with as there are land mines everywhere.

Retaining customers in business is energy efficient. It takes one-tenth the resources to keep a client as it does to find a new one. The average dissatisfied customer will tell nine to ten other people. Thirteen percent of unhappy customers will tell 20 other people. Customers who complain and have their complaint resolved only tell five other people. In business about 96% of unsatisfied customers never make a formal complaint. And 90% of these unhappy customers never return.

A business or industry provides a specific product or service. It affects a single facet of most people's lives. When you go to the gas station to buy gas, it is 15 minutes out of your day. If you go to the grocery store it's 30 minutes out of your day. If the grocery store doesn't have what you want, you go to another one. Businesses and their services and products, especially with the internet, are things we can pick and choose. We can stop going to one dry cleaner and just go to another. Business owners know this, so resolving customer complaints is very important.

In primary relationships however, it's more complicated. First of all, a relationship with a spouse or significant other impacts our life far more than 10-30 minutes a day. There are weeks when we're on vacation, when they may impact all of our time. Many important decisions need to be made with a life partner. Decisions like where to live, how many children to have, what pets to own, what cars to buy, etc. impact our lives every day.

Healthy relationships have times of discomfort. Each partner will have personal growing pains, disappointments, challenges and times of self-doubt. Loving connected partners stay emotionally available even when there is nothing they can do to resolve their loved one's issue. The ability to be present and support the other while they're struggling with a problem is real partnership. This requires not taking it personally when the one you love is struggling, and remembering you can't fix it.

Often, one partner will experience great discomfort when their beloved is not happy. Whether this discomfort is about them, the relationship or some other situation in life doesn't seem to matter. When couples are very close, they can actually feel the emotional pain the other is experiencing. If they're not strong and can't handle the separateness a personal struggle can bring, they can become anxious and demand their loved one get out of pain as soon as possible. This is done with the best of intentions, but it comes across as a demand.

 At the beginning of many relationships there's a sensitivity and concern to the other being mad or disappointed. As a relationship grows, there tends to be more expressions of agitation and frustration when the other is upset or not happy with something about their partner. This desire to quickly have the other in a happy place again can be motivated by many things. One may be the fear that the other will make them responsible for their discomfort. A partner may be concerned that their loved one's unhappiness may damper their own plans. A partner may be afraid that every sign of discontentment is a sign that the relationship is in trouble and they need to hurry and "fix" how the other feels before they leave them for someone else.

Even great relationships have ebbs and flows of craving to be together versus being independent and self-sufficient. This reaching toward togetherness and then fleeing from being "suffocated" and pulling away, are normal parts of all relationships.

The degrees to which these swings take place and the subsequent level of pain a couple experiences, has a lot to do with how much this process is honored and how much it is resisted. Trying to chase down a partner who needs some space may make them feel special, or it may make them feel controlled. This is an important aspect of relationship to talk about with your partner, as it may change from one situation to the next.

It can become contentious if couples see this normal ambivalence in relationships as something that needs to be "fixed." Fights can start by one partner chasing the other, who is just trying to balance this ever changing paradox within themselves. The pursued partner then creates even more distance, trying to create peace within themselves.

This happens on an unconscious level and it can take a lot of personal awareness to be able to talk openly about it. What's important to note is that rushing to make a partner comfortable may be received as patronizing. This is not to say that your partner doesn't need compassion and your loving presence when they're sad, angry, disappointed, or frightened. Just remember that not all discomfort in your relationship needs an immediate fix. In fact, the things we struggle with in our innermost selves usually do not have quick fixes. Rather, they urge us to grow beyond where we were before and step up into a new expanded definition of ourselves. This is personal growth, where we see ourselves as stronger, more capable, etc.

Some couples I see tend to view issues in black and white and in all or none terms. These tend to be individuals with addictions or who grew up in addictive or abusive households where there was little tolerance for stress. Addicts learn at the time they begin using their drug of choice, that tension can be quickly, artificially lowered for a while. Those who grew up in addictive or abusive households also learned that tension in the air could be emotionally or physically dangerous, so finding ways to calm things down as fast as possible meant safety. Both addicts and children raised in unsafe environments, have unconscious triggers to try to get conflict ended as quickly as possible. Many of these couples show signs of physical and emotional stress when there's not a quick fix to be found during a conflict, so they will often try anything to close the emotional distance in the relationship. They may resort to anger or threats of leaving to try to get their partner to get over it. Every fight seems like it could be the last. In the midst of an argument, it feels that if the other person doesn't understand, the relationship will be over *that day*. It's as if all decisions are immediate issues that will mean the difference between staying in business or not. *Everything* seems to be riding on calming down the upset person.

The terror that every fight may be the last drives many couples. This is one of the reasons some couples have such a hard time developing skills that are not outcome-focused. To stay focused on the present, and calmly discuss feelings and wants is terrifying. It feels like a waste of time. at any moment the scales may tilt, and their partner will decide *this* really was the last straw, and now they'll leave.

When couples have been fighting like this for years several things happen. First, the *seriousness* each person brings to the fight, becomes very important. If one partner doesn't take the topic *du jour very* seriously, obviously they don't care about the relationship. Any show of respectful calmness may draw an accusation of apathy. If they really cared, they'd be more engaged over this serious topic that could ruin the relationship.

Secondly, the intensity of these arguments becomes addicting. Each partner gets to feel special because the other would spend so much time and emotion trying to reconnect with them (no matter how verbally abusive it gets). This intensity has chemical components in the body. People can actually become addicted to the adrenalin and cortisol rushes that the fear and anxiety produce. This may seem sad, but many couples thrive on the tension and passion created by conflict. They may actually feel loved that their partner would put so much effort into saving the relationship. In fact when other coping skills are learned in therapy, they may discontinue therapy because everything feels flat. They miss the intensity that comes with fighting and the adrenalin. They may quit therapy or find another therapist who will allow them to keep fighting with the intensity they desire.

Thirdly, partners who are in this immediacy pattern feel very replaceable. They feel every part of the relationship is up for grabs. They have come to believe they are irreparably broken and no one else would want them. Until these partners can forgive themselves for whatever they feel their fatal flaw might be, it will be hard for them to stand outside the need to fight for the relationship.

When couples are very close they are sensitive to *any* emotional distance between them. It can feel scary and lonely if your partner is going through something painful. It can feel that their suffering is going on too long and there's nothing to do for it. Once again, if there's a safe environment where feelings and desires can safely be spoken about, a partner is less likely to feel abandoned. Letting someone in pain know you see their discomfort and you understand what they'd like, can go a long way toward them feeling supported and not alone.

In business a disgruntled client needs to be addressed quickly. Fix it if you can, make it right if it's at all possible. In primary relationships however, acknowledging the pain, showing compassion for the discomfort and letting your partner know you care are far more important. Even if their emotional struggle is about your relationship, allowing them space, listening with respect and being responsible for your own feelings are the best gifts you can give.

Dear Larry:

I don't tell you enough how much I love you.
With the traveling we're both doing, I feel like the distance
between us grows without us being fully aware of it, our
relationship dwindling to a series of brief Skype calls or texts.
Then when we get home, we try to pick up where we left off,
but it always feels to me like something's missing. We have the
intimacy, but I think I need to foster my part in it more, even
during the time we're not together.
I don't believe that distance has to mean we're doomed, so I
wanted to reach out to you with this letter and ask if you felt the
same way. (Letters are so romantic and hardly anyone writes to
each other anymore this way, so here you are!)
When I'm away, I think of you constantly, wishing that we were
nearby for all of the obvious reasons—sex, affection, just sitting
on the couch with you —but also because you're important to me.
The time away from each other is also a good thing and I don't
want to diminish it: Our trips, work, new life experiences,
interests...all of these add to my life immeasurably and I'm
grateful for them, even if I feel a little bit jealous about it stealing
time away from us as a couple.
Am I rambling here? I hope not, but before I do, thank you
for being on this journey with me, for being my companion in
exhaustion and time deprivation, but also for being the man I
share my bed and my heart with.

Max

"The capacity to be alone is the capacity to love. It may look
paradoxical to you, but it's not. It is an existential truth: only
those people who are capable of being alone are capable of love,
of sharing, of going into the deepest core of another person--
without possessing the other, without becoming dependent on
the other, without reducing the other to a thing, and without
becoming addicted to the other. They allow the other absolute

freedom, because they know that if the other leaves, they will be as happy as they are now. Their happiness cannot be taken by the other, because it is not given by the other."--Osho

Exercises:

Think back on times you pushed a little too hard to try and make your partner feel better. Remember their reactions. Try and recall how you felt. What were the things you did to cope with your discomfort while they worked things out in their mind? How did you eventually reconnect?

Board Room:
"If we separate, that's it. I'm filing for divorce."
"You're always unhappy. Why don't you just look at the good side of things once in a while?"
"If it's so stressful, quit!"
"You think you had it tough today! Let me tell you about my day, it was much worse!"
"I'll speak to you when you're reasonable!"

Bedroom:
"I'm very afraid of a separation. I'm scared I'm not that important to you and you'll find you're happier without me. I want us to spend time together whether we're under one roof or two."
"We both have had rough days! I'd like it if we could both just sit on the couch and cuddle and tell each other about our day."
"I miss you. I'd like to put a romantic date on the calendar."

Written Exercises:

Write a paragraph describing how you feel when your partner is upset, disappointed, angry or hurt.
Write a paragraph about what you're afraid will happen when your partner is upset.
Write a list of five things you can do to keep yourself centered and not need to "rush in" and make your partner feel better.

Chapter Thirty-six

WAYS TO REKINDLE ROMANCE AND INCORPORATE FEELINGS AND WANTS

"All she wanted was a family, all he wanted was fame; as their relationship famished."
— Anthony Liccione

"Be not afraid of growing slowly, be afraid only of standing still." — *Chinese Proverb*

When a couple stops selling each other on feelings and desires, magic happens. When we know we have a loving caring person who'll stand beside us, however slow or fast we learn our lessons, then we feel free to follow our dreams and play full out.

When we accept our own feelings (comfortable or uncomfortable ones) and we embrace our dreams (both the attainable and the impossible ones) we then have the ability to accept these in our partner.

When energy is expended trying to defend one's feelings and substantiate their right to have a dream, a great deal of valuable energy is lost. Many people who waste proving feelings and wants to each other never have the energy to create and contribute to the world the talents they have to offer.

By focusing on *process* and being fully present with each other, in pain or in happiness, a couple gives the world a tremendous gift of vitality and joy. Don't underestimate the far-extending ripple effect creating peace and connection in your relationship can have. Beyond being role models for your children, you touch lives you will never know about. We're not islands. How we feel, what we want, how we treat ourselves and our partner matters.

The paradox is, if we *try* to have this outcome by defending our right to have it, or by convincing our partner it's important, it will allude us. By embracing the moment, the feelings, the hungers, the dreams in each and every day, we're actually creating an environment in which our highest dreams can be born. Work on the environment, the outcome will take care of itself.

If you don't know where to start, begin with journaling about your own feelings and wants. Firstly, learn how to label your feelings of sadness, ambivalence, discontentment, etc.

Then journal about what you want. In the next hour, in the next day, week, month, six months, year, five years, and ten years. If you don't know what you want, there's no way you can share your dreams with your partner. Ask yourself what you want educationally, financially, for vacations, holidays, breakfast, what to wear, experience, explore. These do not need to be 10's on a scale of 1-10; they might be 2s or 4s. It's okay to write down small wants and almost imperceptible feelings. They *are* wants and feelings, too.

After you've written about these for a few weeks, write down the ones you'd like to share with your partner. If you feel safer, give them to him/her in writing. Ask them if they understand them. Have them acknowledge each one, either in writing or verbally. Ask for acknowledgement of your feelings and wants before your partner shares theirs. Make sure after they share that you also acknowledge the feelings and wants that have been shared with you.

Remember if you're a little wobbly at first, cut each other some slack. Here's an example:

Tyler: "When I get home the TV is always on."
Angela: "How do you feel about that?"
Tyler: "Well, I wish you would turn it off."
Angela: "OK, your want is for me to turn
it off. How do you feel about it?"

Tyler: "I feel like you are talking in circles. You
know what I want, what more is there to it?"
Angela: "There is the feeling part. It sounds to me like
you are feeling agitated at this conversation."
Tyler: "BINGO, Yeah, I'm agitated."
Angela: "You want to know how I feel and what I want?"
Tyler: "Sure, why not?"
Angela: "I want to know when you are unhappy about
things like the TV. I want to be the person you tell things
to when you are agitated. I feel close to you when you do
these boring talking exercises with me." Tyler: "Sure."
Angela: "Would you please just repeat back what I said,
so I know you heard me. I really would like that."
Tyler: "You want to know when I'm complaining about something
and you feel close to me when we do these boring exercises."
Angela: "Well, Close enough. Thank you. I love you."

If you can, start with keeping the conversation simple. Stay away
from outcome or substantiating facts. It may not sound like a
flowing conversation. It may sound stilted and unnatural. Anything
we do for the first few times---especially if we're countering years
of old communication habits--- will seem strange and unnatural.
Be patient with yourself. Each time you have an interaction and
it doesn't lead to trying to change each other, you've successfully
added to the foundation of building trust and closeness. The next
time a difficult topic arises, it will be easier. Trust that you can
contribute to a safe, respectful conversation between you and your
partner.

Even though the previous interaction may not have been all that
warm and intimate, the conversation could've gone like this:

Tyler: "When I get home the TV is always on."
Angela: "It's not always on. I was gone yesterday
when you got home. The day before that, my niece
was over and she likes watching Disney videos."
Tyler: "Can't I ever come home to a quiet house?"
Angela: (Realizing nothing about feelings or wants is getting

discussed) "*How do you feel about coming home to a noisy house?*"
Tyler: "I feel like you've been reading too many self-help books! Where's the paper?"
Angela: (Remembering that no feeling statement ever starts with "I feel like you...") "How do you really feel?"
Tyler: "Leave me alone. You know how I feel!"
Angela: "How would I know how you feel? You think everyone can read your mind! You're always complaining that we aren't close enough and you want more sex. Well if you don't start treating me with more respect, it will be a lot longer! You think the whole world revolves around you! Tomorrow, I'll make sure the TV and the stereo is on!"

Conversations based on facts and evidence quickly deteriorate. When discussions aren't focus on feelings and wants, control and outcome issues get in the way.

Be gentle with yourself. Remember there are not many models of how to talk clearly and straightforwardly about your inner self. Developing a vocabulary about how you feel and ways to describe the things you want is one of the best gifts you can give your relationship.

Practice in writing if it feels "too charged" to start verbally. Keep a sense of humor. Taking life too seriously can easily get in the way of being vulnerable.

Examples of creating closeness by sharing feelings and wants:
1. Write a paragraph recalling how you felt when the two of you first met. (Be specific, i.e. "I felt butterflies in my stomach," "I felt scared you wouldn't go out with me," "I was nervous about your friends not liking me," etc.) Add details about the things you liked, the hopes and dreams you had and the things you wanted ("I was hoping you'd look over at me." "I wanted you to go with me to the party." "I was hoping we'd end up in the same group.") Leave it on his/her mirror, car seat or pillow.
2. Create envelopes with activities you know he/she has wanted

227

to do or experience. Drive to a quiet place together, pull out three or four sealed envelopes, have them open the envelope of their choice and read the agenda for the evening: Dinner and a movie; your favorite juice bar and a comedy club, or Chinese take-out at the park and then listening to music at a coffee house. Ask if this is something he/she they would want to do. If not, have them draw another envelope.

3. Many times in our busy days, compliments get neglected in a primary relationship. There is a way to give compliments in a way that really matters: in writing. It takes some vulnerability to write a compliment because it could be held against you later, i.e. "I thought you liked the way I wore my hair!" Write 31 things you admire about your partner, put them in a decorative container and have them read one every morning for a month.

4. Choose a song that expresses how you feel. Have your partner sit quietly with you and listen to the song together. State specifically how the song reflects how you feel and what you wanted them to know about that.

5. Being happy in partnership is about feeling that you have an impact on the other person's life. When we get caught up in the fast pace of life we sometimes forget what things would be like without this partner. Putting words to how you feel lucky is one of the most powerful things you can do in a relationship. Write a note stating three ways the world is a better place because he/she is in it. Give the note with a single stem flower and say, "You're one of a kind."

6. Creating feelings of specialness and importance can short-circuit many trivial disagreements. Find ways to let your partner know that they are special and important to you. Such as, using his/her first name to create an acronym with words that describe him/her i.e.; Lisa and Mark:

Loving   Marvelous
Inspiring   Adventurous
Sexy   Rowdy
Adorable   Kind

7. Unconsciously we record a ratio of compliments to criticisms. When the ratio becomes too high in favor of the criticisms, we get defensive, even if what our partner is saying next isn't going

to be a criticism. It's also important to pay attention to how many directives you give proportionally to how many compliments. Say "Thank you." Express gratitude and appreciation often. Be sure to give compliments at least five times as often as criticisms or directives.

8. Creating fun is difficult for many couples. If there's a lot of hostility and tension between you, any attempts at fun may be met with "What do you want from me now?" You may need to walk slowly into creative playfulness, but by all means incorporate it into your life! You can create a romantic treasure hunt with loving notes or gifts at each stop and riddles that point to the next location. Have the final destination be a quiet restaurant, candle-lit bubble bath, or a massage in bed with warmed oil.

9. Remember that intimacy may mean different things to men and women. Read John Gray's *Men Are From Mars, Women Are From Venus* aloud to each other. Respectfully talk about what makes each of you feel close to the other. Remember, feeling safe and unconditionally accepted leads both men and women to feel loved and special.

10. Allow yourself to be vulnerable. Gently and directly reveal how you feel and what you want. Comment aloud on the things they do that lead you to feel special and important to them. Give yourself the right to own your feelings and dreams without justification or providing "evidence." If you're comfortable with how you feel and what you want, others will also be more comfortable with you.

In twenty years, you and I will:

1) Be slightly heavier. I think there's no way around that.
2) Still struggle with money but be financially secure enough to enjoy retirement.
3) Write and paint and create more beautiful things.
4) Dance in the living room to Hits of the 80s. (Even the bad ones.)
5) Read more books.
6) Travel to London and see plays.
7) Watch less TV.
8) Eat no fast food (except In 'N Out if they're still around).
9) Speak French.

10) Have a backyard, so that we can have a dog.

Exercises:
Think of a creative way to be romantic with your partner.

Board Room:
"No one makes any money doing *that*."
"You are just trying to stay away from home and avoid your responsibilities here!"
"There's no way you should want that.
Think of what it will cost us!"
"I've already sacrificed enough, and now you want more! Why don't you just let someone else take care of that?"

Bedroom:
"I don't understand why you'd want to take on
that challenge, but I support you in it."
"I'm scared when you talk about that. I'm afraid there won't be enough time, money, energy, and I'll have full responsibility for the kids. Would you be willing to talk with me about each of my fears? I don't need answers this minute, but I'd like to know we can talk about this. I'm afraid I'll end up feeling lonely."
"I'd like to know your dream that seems to be
pulling at you. Can you describe what it looks like?
I promise to be accepting and not judge it."

Optional Exercises:

Share a journal or email account with your
partner. Write back and forth to each other.

Chapter Thirty-seven

AN EXERCISE FOR COUPLES

"Someone to tell it to is one of the fundamental needs
of human beings."
— Miles Franklin

This exercise, as the others in this book, may seem contrived and "not how anyone really talks." However, if you learn to use the principles demonstrated here, you'll be able to have conversations that can build closeness and connection.

A good way to begin is to set aside time (10-15 min.) where you won't be interrupted. Agree on when you'll meet to practice ahead of time so it doesn't feel like you're sabotaging your partner.

Keep your sentences short. It will be easier for you partner to repeat them back if they're short. Remember, *no* feeling ever starts with "I feel like you---" Use real feeling words that tell how you really feel inside. Self-revealing is the purpose here, not blaming, so reveal the emotions that you most want *seen*.

When you share what you want, be as specific as possible. It's easier for your partner to really get a picture of what you want if you're concise and specific. For example, "I want you to understand me" is vague. "I want you to look into my eyes when we're talking and turn the TV off," is something observable, so it's easier to acknowledge.

It's all right to bring up uncomfortable feelings that seem to have no real solutions. And it's all right to express desires you think can't ever rally happen such as: "I'm really sad." "What I'd like is to turn back the clock and make last year never happen."

Sharing grief, regret and other things that can't be "fixed" can still bring you closer together. Just remember that you're each responsible for your own feelings. Repeating back what the other says is a way of acknowledging feelings, even grief, and letting your partner know you care and will stay fully present with them. (Remember the labor analogy and how important it is to just stay present).

Decide who is A and who is B. Smile, it's not all *that* serious!

Partner A starts by saying and completing the first statement.

A: "Right now I'm feeling---"

B: (looking into A's eyes) repeats back what A said.

A: "And what I'd like from you about that is---"

B: Once again repeats what A said. Then it's B's turn.

B: "When I hear you say that, I feel---"

A: repeats back what B said (continuing to look into B's eyes)

B: And what I'd like about that is---"

And once again A repeats back what B says.

Then A says again: "When I hear you say that I feel---"

B repeats it back.

A says: "And what I'd like about that is..."

No "Because---" statements. If you're defending why you feel a certain way, or that you have a right to feel however you feel, you're not giving yourself the right to feel and want without substantiation.

This exercise is difficult to do at first. Most couples have a hard time staying focused on this process without drifting into "What are we going to do about this?" Resisting the urge to substantiate how you feel and justify what you want with logic goes against everything you've probably practiced for years! Be gentle with yourselves, but whichever one of you catches the conversation drifting into old communication patterns or heading toward a solution, redirect it back to the exercise.

B repeats back and then says "When I hear you say that I feel---"

A repeats it back.

Then B says: And what I would like about that is---"

And A repeats it back.

Continue this process until you can stay focused on the statements in the moment. If the conversation becomes redundant reveal more deeply about how you feel and share your vulnerable wishes.

Here's how Daniel and Rebekah did the exercise.

Rebekah: "Right now, I'm feeling silly."
Daniel: "Right now, you are feeling silly."
Rebekah: What I would like about that is for
you to tell me I am not looking foolish."
Daniel: "And what you would like about that is
for me to tell you that you don't look foolish. And
when I hear you say that, I feel defensive."
Rebekah (looking surprised): "And when you
hear me say that, you feel defensive."
Daniel: And what I would like about that is for you
to care so much about our relationship that you
weren't worried about how you looked."
Rebekah (a little frustrated): "And what you would
like about that is for me to care so much about the
relationship that I wouldn't care if I looked foolish.

233

And when I hear you say that, I feel angry."
Daniel: "And when you hear me say that, you feel angry."
Rebekah: "And what I would like about that is for
you to be able to handle my nervousness without
drawing conclusions about my priorities."

Daniel: "And what you would like is for me to handle
your nervousness and not draw conclusions about your
priorities. And when I hear you say that, I feel confused."
Rebekah: "And when you hear me say that you feel confused."
Daniel (gazing into Rebecca's eyes): "And
what I would like about that is for you to tell
me I am important and special to you."
Rebekah (tearing up a little): "And what you want is for me
to tell you, you are special and important to me. And when
I hear you say that, I feel hopeful and close to you."
Daniel: "And when you hear me say that,
you feel hopeful and close to me."
Rebekah: "And what I want you to know is that
you are very special and important to me!"
Daniel: "And what you want me to know is that I
am very special and important to you. And when I
hear you say that I feel happy and relieved."
Rebekah: "And when you hear me say that,
you feel happy and relieved."
Daniel: "And what I want about this is to be able to talk this way
without interrupting each other and with no defensiveness."
Rebekah (trying to remember all he said): "And what you want
is for us to talk without interrupting and without defensiveness.
And when I hear you say that, I feel hopeful and close to you."
Daniel: "And when you hear me say that,
you feel hopeful and close to me."

Exercises:

Notice throughout the day how you *feel* and
what you'd *want* at the moment.

234

Optional Exercises:

If trying to pin your partner down to a time to practice the above exercise seems unlikely, or too vulnerable, you can email or text him/her with similar exchanges. Remember the goal is to keep the conversation confined to each of your feelings and wants, without evidence and story-telling. Remember to let each other know you actually heard what the other said before you disclose your own feelings and desires. Doing this exercise by phone may work better for some couples. On the phone you have fewer cues to avoid responding to (no visuals, rolled eyes, eyes dilating, sweating, wringing hands etc.)

Proof

Made in the USA
Charleston, SC
16 January 2016